FIRST WORLD, HA HA HA!
THE ZAPATISTA CHALLENGE

EDITED BY ELAINE KATZENBERGER

CITY LIGHTS
SAN FRANCISCO

Cover photograph by Ignacio Nuñez Pliego
Cover design by Rex Ray
Book design by Elaine Katzenberger
Typography by Harvest Graphics
All photos and illustrations © the individual artists

Library of Congress Cataloging-in-Publication Data

First World, ha ha ha! The Zapatista Challenge / edited by Elaine
Katzenberger
      p.   cm.
    ISBN 0-87286-294-1 : $12.95
     1. Chiapas (Mexico) — History — Peasant Uprising, 1994.
  2. Mexico — Politics and government — 1988-   3. Ejército Zapatista de
Liberación Nacional (Mexico) 4. Subcomandante Marcos. 5. Mexico
— Relations — United States. 6. United States — Relations — Mexico.
I. Katzenberger, Elaine.
F1256.F57 1995
940.55'9 — dc20
                                               94-31873
                                               CIP

City Lights Books are available to bookstores through our primary
distributor: Subterranean Company, P.O. Box 160, 265 S. 5th St., Monroe,
OR 97456. 503-847-5274. Toll-free orders 800-274-7826. FAX 503-847-6018.
Our books are also available through library jobbers and regional distributors.
For personal orders and catalogs, please write to City Lights Books,
261 Columbus Avenue, San Francisco, CA 94133.

CITY LIGHTS BOOKS are edited by Lawrence Ferlinghetti and Nancy J.
Peters and published at the City Lights Bookstore, 261 Columbus Avenue,
San Francisco, CA 94133.

ACKNOWLEDGMENTS

I would like to thank the following people for their support, advice, and enthusiasm for this project: Juvenal Acosta, Elva Macías, Vivian Newdick, Nancy J. Peters, Greg Ruggiero, Stuart Sahulka and Amy Scholder.

"Overheard in the Marketplace" (originally titled *Testimonios*) and "Chamula Carnaval" were published in *La Jicara*, a journal from San Cristóbal, Chiapas.

"It Comes From Afar," and "Galloping Into the Future" originally appeared in Mexico's national newspaper, *La Jornada*.

"Time Bombs" was published in *In These Times*, Feb. 21, 1994.

"Seeds of a Revolt" originally appeared in *Commonweal Magazine*, Winter 1994.

"Interview: Indigenous and Campesino Council of Chiapas" was published (originally titled "Interview with Antonio Hernández Cruz of CIOAC") in *Abya Yala News*, Vol. 8, Nos. 1 & 2, Summer, 1994.

"Living Conditions," "Land," "Religion & Expulsions" all appeared in an article entitled, "Chronicle of a conflict foretold" by Elsa Montiel in *Voices of Mexico*, No. 27, June, 1994.

The "Statement of Support" by Leonard Peltier was provided by the International Action Coalition in New York, sponsors of the CONAC-EZLN's speaking tour of the U.S. in May, 1994.

In the Introduction, Paul Goodman is quoted from *Speaking and Language: a Defence of poetry* (Random House, 1971).

The epigraph for this book is an excerpt from Adrienne Rich's essay, "The hermit's scream," published in a collection entitled, *What Is Found There; Notebooks on Poetry and Politics* (Norton, 1993).

TRANSLATIONS

This book would not have been possible without the work of the following translators, whose interest and expertise added a great deal to this project (credits are indicated by the translator's initials, which appear at the end of each selection):

SYLVIA MULLALY AGUIRRE
ANNUAR MURRAR
BARBARA PASCHKE
MARGOT PEPPER
CLIFTON ROSS

When we do and think and feel certain things privately and in secret, even when thousands of people are doing, thinking, whispering these things privately and in secret, there is still no general, collective understanding from which to move. Each takes her or his own risks in isolation. We may think of ourselves as individual rebels, and individual rebels can easily be shot down. The relationship among so many feelings remains unclear. But these thoughts and feelings, suppressed and stored-up and whispered, have an incendiary component. You cannot tell where or how they will connect, spreading underground from rootlet to rootlet till every grass blade is afire from every other. This is that "spontaneity" that party "leaders," secret governments, and closed systems dread.

— *Adrienne Rich*

CONTENTS

INTRODUCTION

> ... it is not only by shooting bullets in the battlefields that
> tyranny is overthrown, but also by hurling ideas of redemption,
> words of freedom and terrible anathemas against the hangmen
> that people bring down dictators and empires ...
>
> — Emiliano Zapata

In early January of 1994, the story from Chiapas and the photos of Zapatistas were accompanied by the following headline in the *San Francisco Examiner*: "Roots of Rebellion: Poverty and Oppression." What could have provoked this sudden outburst of political truth on the front page? Somehow, it seemed, a popular uprising in Mexico was commanding center stage in a sympathetic light. From here, it seemed like a glimmer of hope.

When the Zapatista Army emerged from the jungle, "the ones without faces, the ones without voices" stepped directly into the media spotlight, making front page news around the world. During the occupation of San Cristóbal, spokesperson and military strategist Subcomandante Marcos declared their subversive intention: "We want to know what this event will provoke, what will move the national consciousness." Having won access to the international press and communications media, the Zapatistas used them to wage a parallel war of words and symbols, an effective decolonization of public language. Their Declaration of War was an emotional appeal to the conscience and frustrated electoral desires of the nation; and it was broadcast on the radio, read on national television, and faxed to the Mexican and international press.

The Mexican government's initial response was predictable: an attempt to discredit the movement as the work of outsiders who were manipulating the (admittedly) poverty-stricken native populations and using them to destabilize the country. The army was sent out to crush the uprising.

Public sympathy for the Zapatistas was immediate and overwhelming. Demonstrators filled plazas throughout the country — and in many foreign cities as well — holding banners that read, "We are all Chiapanecos." It soon became apparent that the government would be forced to acquiesce to the growing international demand for a cease-fire. A sense of shared triumph began to spread. On the day that the official cease-fire was declared, there was a large demonstration in Mexico City. Over 100,000 people marched together, shouting, "First World, Ha Ha Ha!" in open defiance of the ruling class and its economic allies in "developed" countries to the North, who were opening Mexico to foreign investment. It was an expression of solidarity with the Zapatistas, who had repudiated the official facade of political stability and economic well-being in Mexico. And it was the catharsis of exposing and acknowledging the actual conditions of worsening poverty and repression, and publicly naming the cause for them.

The ability to provoke an understanding of common struggle among diverse peoples was the most striking aspect of the Zapatista insurrection. Commandeering technology and language that had been formatted to occlude them, the Zapatistas positioned themselves as the heirs of the Mexican people's historic struggle for democracy and justice. They linked the national and native hearts of Mexico, and a public, collective soul-searching ensued. Questions of self-perception and self-representation — as a people, as a society, and as a nation — filled the pages of the Mexican press. It was, as Juan Bañuelos writes, ". . . the confrontation between two designs for living: the indigenous way of *being* and *fulfillment*, and the neoliberal way of *possession* and *power*." It created a brief, unsettled, hopeful period, one that Guillermo Gómez Peña describes as, ". . . a time in which we all experimented with the realm of unlimited utopian possibilities." And this collective response to the Zapatista challenge has changed Mexico, despite the government's attempts to preserve appearances.

This book was conceived as a way to translate, broadcast, and amplify the sense of possibility that was created by the uprising. It presents diverse writings and viewpoints from Mexico, including first-hand testimonies by Zapatista villagers, soldiers, and leaders, and interviews with members of campesino, indigenous, and women's organizations who live and work in the area of conflict. Eraclio Zepeda, Juan Bañuelos, Elva Macías and Efraín Bartolomé — all internationally known poets from Chiapas — give moving and personal responses to the crisis. Mexico City writers — Elena Poniatowska, Mongo Sánchez Lira, Rogelio Villarreal, and Guillermo Gómez Peña — offer urban perspectives that illustrate the Zapatista movement's broader connections and impact within Mexico, and the psychological and cultural distances it travelled.

Political analysts, historians, and journalists — Antonio García de León, Blanche Petrich, Peter Rosset and John Ross — establish the background and context for the rebellion: the history of indigenous resistance and the struggle for land, the legacy of Emiliano Zapata and the Revolution of 1910, and Mexico's deteriorating political and economic conditions.

First World, HA HA HA! also examines the resonance of the Zapatista uprising outside of Mexico, where the insurrection was widely hailed as a direct attack on the New World Order. In the post-Cold War era, with global economic restructuring — codified in treaties such as NAFTA and GATT — the Zapatista rebellion made it clear that the battle lines are now more clearly drawn. Writers from the United States explore the nature of this new development, and its potential for social movements here in our country. Noam Chomsky demonstrates that "nationality" is meaningless to an economic alliance which has no boundaries, and Iain Boal observes, "The resistance will be as transnational as capital."

Native people in all of the Americas understood the rebellion as a continuation of the historic indigenous resistance of the hemisphere. Native writers and activists from both Mexico and the United States link the Zapatista movement to a continental — and worldwide — struggle for indigenous rights. Ward Churchill states, " . . . the Zapatistas — and the *indigenismo* they incarnate — represent the revitalization of revolutionary potential . . . in ways which finally and truly *do* lead toward self-determination for all peoples, no matter how small or 'primitive' . . ."

In the United States, we are conditioned to believe that popular struggle cannot succeed. The press is widely employed to maintain a state of political hopelessness; we have become used to what Paul Goodman describes as "format": "Format is not like censorship that tries to obliterate speech, and so sometimes empowers it by making it important. And it is not like propaganda that simply tells lies. . . . Format is speech colonized, broken-spirited. . . . The government of a complicated modern society cannot lie *much.* But by format, even without trying, it can kill feeling, memory, learning, observation, imagination, [and] logic . . . " This is the formula that enables us to accept the increasing number of people with signs reading, "Hungry. Please help."

As the economic situation worsens, laws are created to criminalize such behavior as sitting or sleeping on sidewalks, and prisons and law-enforcement are given priority in the national budget. We are being led into complicity in our own repression. Noam Chomsky writes, "A few days after the NAFTA vote, the

U.S. Senate passed . . . legislation call[ing] for 100,000 new police, high-security regional prisons, boot camps for young offenders, extension of the death penalty and harsher sentencing, as well as other onerous measures. . . . The concept of 'efficiency,' as defined by those of wealth and privilege, offers nothing to the growing sectors of the population that are useless for profit-making, and thus have been driven to poverty and despair. If they cannot be confined to urban slums, they will have to be controlled in some other way."

The rebellion in Los Angeles was the most recent large-scale popular uprising in our country. It was given the familiar context of interracial antagonism in the media, although the scenes of massive looting pointed to other frustrations. The implied story was the shared anger of Los Angeles's poor, who were turning not against each other but against the symbols of their economic oppression. The coalitions that were formed in the wake of the violence have endured a concerted campaign of repression by the police, but most people are unaware of their existence and struggle. The collective memory of what happened in Los Angeles remains one of races at war, senseless violence, and people wreaking havoc until order was restored by the federal government. The underlying causes for the poverty which fueled the uprising were never widely perceived or discussed in the media, and American society has yet to find a way to unmask our own concealed truths.

In California's elections of 1994, a proposition that would deny social services to illegal immigrants was passed after heated debate. Alternative solutions to the "immigration problem" were discussed in the media, by politicians, and on the street. Most liberals seemed to favor the more "humane" approach, namely, reinforcing the border to make it impenetrable. (Immigrants from Mexico constitute the majority of "illegal aliens" in the state.) Of course, there was no public mention — except by

Latinos — that California and the entire Southwest had been stolen from Mexico by force (and from Native Americans before that), and that the definition of "illegal immigrant" is an insult to the original inhabitants of this land. Low wages, unemployment, poverty, and immigration were not perceived as the effects of an intentional, international policy — NAFTA and GATT did not figure in the discussion.

Pete Wilson, the governor who had based his reelection campaign on this piece of legislation celebrated his victory saying that he figured, "all those people will just have to go back where they came from." A few days later, the *New York Times* reported the following election-day protest:

"About 40 masked men ransacked a McDonald's restaurant in Mexico City today to protest a ballot proposal in California that would cut social benefits of illegal immigrants and their families.

'The assailants broke windows, threw cash registers to the floor, overturned wastebaskets and painted graffiti denouncing the United States in the restaurant in the fashionable Zona Rosa area of the capital,' said a McDonald's marketing manager, Manuel Juárez. He said no one was injured.

'Yankee Go Home!' 'Solidarity With the Immigrants!' and 'No to 187!' were among the messages scrawled on the restaurant's windows. . . . McDonald's is viewed by many Mexican leftists as a symbol of American imperialism." The report goes on to say that the Mexican federal police were called in to defend the Golden Arches against the angry demonstrators.

In his address to the Democratic National Convention which was convened by the Zapatistas in the jungle of Chiapas and attended by 6,000 activists and intellectuals, Subcomandante Marcos said, "We direct ourselves to this Convention, to ask in the name of all men and women . . . that you save a moment, a few days, a few hours, enough minutes to find the common enemy." Until quite recently, people in the so-called First World

— the United States in particular — have been comfortably unaware of the "common enemy," and resistance struggles have been waged on the margins of society. As the situation worsens for the majority of people, there is the hope that societies will look for actual alternatives, and that the search will transcend national borders.

This book is a chronicle of societal transformation, a look at what happens when the hope for change is ignited. The Zapatista rebellion has not ended, and Mexico continues to be shaken by it. As Octavio Paz wrote in 1972, "Zapata is beyond the controversy between liberals and conservatives, Marxists and neocapitalists: Zapata is *before* — and perhaps, if Mexico is not extinguished, he will be *after*." The Zapatistas' successful entry into the national — and international — consciousness holds promise for the struggle for social justice everywhere. As Ronnie Burk writes, "At the end of this mad century of revolutions, Mexico might very well show the world how it's done."

— E.K.

OVERHEARD IN THE MARKETPLACE

Munda Tostón

IT ALL STARTED ONE TUESDAY IN MAY.

As usual, I was in my little spot in the marketplace when a young Chamula girl came up to me, asking for ski masks.

"How many do you want?" I asked her.

"How many do you have?"

"Well, I don't know how many you need; I have thirty here."

She paid for all thirty and ordered three hundred more. I ordered ten gross of ski masks from Puebla, and she bought all of them from me. This was in May.

In June, some others came to buy green pants. They arrived with their lists: fifty pairs of 28" waist, sixty 29", seventy 30", like that. Green pants were in fashion. Lots of business in green pants.

In July they wanted brown shirts. Two hundred size 14, three hundred 14½, four hundred size 15. In August, it's bandanas. The same.

Then in October, November, when it starts to get cold, they come for the heavy shirts. I'd start out in the morning with sixty, and by the afternoon they'd all be gone. It was like that every day. I was selling to them for thirty-five a piece, but then I started to raise the price. "I'm sorry, they'll cost you forty-five now." They bought them all from me anyway. I raised them to fifty, sixty, up to seventy-five. And it went well for me. I finished out the year well, thank God.

The first of January, I'm on my way to open up for business, to see if I can sell a little. But there's no one in the marketplace. "Everyone's at the park," the man who sweeps up tells me.

In order to sell, you have to go where the people are. So I make up my bundle with everything I have to sell, and get myself over to the park.

And there they all are, my clientele, in the City Hall, wearing my green pants, my brown shirts, with the bandana and ski mask.

Since then, I haven't sold a thing.

⁓

Although she doesn't deserve it, the ungrateful little Indian, I always give my girl her Christmas bonus. Like everyone who works on the ranches, she spends it on clothes to take back to her town to sell. I try to help her, so she'll learn how to buy.

"Oh dear," I tell her when she leaves the shop with a dozen shirts, "get a better selection. Look, they're all green. They're not going to buy them from you like that."

"Doña Zola," the ungrateful one answers me, "in January I won't be working anymore."

"What is it, are you getting married, girl? And you just started working — ," but she cuts me off quickly, saying she doesn't have a boyfriend.

"Then what is it you're planning on doing?"

"It's going to be a surprise. You'll see, ma'am."

EK

WAR DIARY
Efraín Bartolomé

IT'S 8:57 A.M. ON THE FIRST OF JANUARY, 1994. MY father wakes me with the news: "The town has been taken; the Zapatista Army for National Liberation has declared war on Salinas."

Disbelief.

I get up, dress myself. My wife turns on the radio: the local station has been converted to "Radio Zapata," where a man with a Central American accent is reading a "Declaration of War Against the Federal Army." An unbroken silence covers the town.

My father says the guerrilleros have already gone down our street, "armed with some pretty good machine guns." Meanwhile, the Declaration of the Lacandón Jungle continues. I'm still not fully awake.

What is this?

The final "l" reverberates in the throat of this revolutionary radio announcer when he says: "*el Ejército Zapatista de Liberación Nacionallll . . . .*"

9:12

We're in the bedroom on the second floor, where we've been sleeping while here on this visit. We go out onto the rooftop that overlooks the street, and through binoculars we can see a man in blue on the roof of City Hall. The radio is playing "The International" in an unrecognizable language. Russian? The short station breaks are filled with the "revolutionary music" we suffered through in the seventies.

9:17

My niece Teté (nine years old) runs up the stairs and tells me to come down, that an armed group is coming by Aristedes's house, on the corner. I go out the door and see a small group approaching, ten or twelve, and another group on the corner.

The assault on the presidency begins. Sporadic, isolated flashes and gunshots. The radio announcer begins to read the "War Tax Law."

My initial impression of the occupation of the town as an innocent strike begins to crumble — the image of the university "islands" in 1971 comes back to me: incendiary discourse of the ultraleftists; the ousting of the university president; the normalists, Fidel y Castro Bustos, Raúl León de la Selva; the PA system turned up as high as it could go; exploding firecrackers electrifying the air.

The War Tax Law. "They've repeated it a few times already," says my brother-in-law Génner.

More gunshots.

A man in a black hat, with an impressive-looking piece of radio equipment, shoots from the corner. What's he shooting at?

6

They're behind barricades on the corner down the street, by my cousin Lety's house, about seven of them. It looks like they're on both sides of the street.

Something explodes and smoke rises near the school. Of course, that's what they're shooting at: the headquarters of the Judicial Police.

What silence now.

9:21

Smoke from the explosion wafts over. It stings my nose and produces tears.

9:23

There are three radios on in the house, and yet, it's the silence in the town that affects me. This is the silence I *used* to hear as a child.

Tears spill from my eyes. I go out onto the terrace that overlooks the garden. The smell and the tears increase. I run downstairs. My wife is giving rags soaked in vinegar and water to the children, covering their noses. There are eight children in the house. Everyone blinks with watery, frightened eyes.

9:30

I go back onto the terrace looking over the street: the small group is still there, but the man with the radio is gone.

Two shots.

9:32

Another explosion and smoke near the church. Of course: the blue uniforms are the Public Security Forces — State Police — guarding City Hall. They're shooting tear gas.

9:36

Ten more shots. The shooting continues. Five now. About fifteen now, from different places.

9:45

Just what we need: José de Molina on the radio in Ocosingo. Never did I imagine that in this unpolluted air . . . "They're going to lose the war with that music," my wife, Pilla, says in a low voice. "No, more like: 'you can have it all, just take off that record,'" I reply.

Why are we talking in whispers?

9:47

Another flash of light.

A truck suddenly appears up the street, coming from the highway. It tries to enter. The people watching at the entrance of the street shout: "What are you going to do here, *hermano?* Don't try it! There's a shoot-out!" The truck stops, the driver talks with the crowd. He throws it into reverse and takes the turnoff to Yajalón.

9:57

Some civilians are in the streets now, walking carefully, like babies taking their first steps, risking it.

My cousins Mario and Ovidio arrive. They signal us from the corner and approach, pressed against the wall. We open the door and they pass through, quickly. They tell us that there are more than a thousand guerrilleros in the town; they've burned down Geofísica (Pemex property) and destroyed three airplanes.

10:00

We talk by the entrance to the patio, filled with cars now — all of my brothers and I are here to celebrate the holidays with my parents. At the end of the patio is the area for hulling coffee beans and the little orchard with lime, orange, coffee, and giant fern trees. The territory of geese, ducks, turkeys, and hens. And seven roosters, for the holidays.

There are seven guerrilleros on the corner. No, six. Eight. It looked like there were more, but now I can only count these. Well-armed. Someone else with a radio arrives. A bunch of them now: they cross the street rapidly.

Now it's clear to me: their objectives are the City Hall and the installations of the Judicial Police. They're converging on them from all parts of town, judging from the shots. "Yes," confirms my cousin Mario, "all the shooting is directed at City Hall. It's crawling with guerrilleros down there."

They asked Mario and Ovidio to join. "They're inviting everyone. Against the rich. 'Don't worry about guns. We'll give them to you.' " I see boots, green pants, brown sweaters or jackets. A red bandana around the neck. Some have black pants. " 'Those who join up will have guns immediately, but if you already have one, so much the better,' someone who talks like a Salvadoreño told us," says Ovidio.

My cousins came from their house on the other side of town to see if we were all right, and to give us the traditional New Year's embrace.

Happy New Year?

The man with the black hat and the big radio antenna reappears on the corner. Completely in black from his boots to his hat. With his red scarf.

People peer out of balconies, doorways, and windows. I've already checked out all the observation points inside the house, and have now gone out onto the sidewalk. Everyone is out taking a little walk, trying to recover a sphere of movement, to reclaim territory abruptly circumscribed to the house by the armed presence. A block up, at the highway, there's a fairly substantial group of watchers, thirty or forty, standing in the middle of the street or sitting on the high sidewalks. They are the owners of buses, or drivers, or passengers who would have traveled today to San Cristóbal or to Palenque. Our house is on the Avenida Central. Given its location, in the high part of town, I have a privileged view of the theater of action.

Mario says that they've done serious damage to the house of Don Enrique Solórzano.

I watch a drunken man crossing the street, staggering, shaking his head "no." He passes between the guerrilleros, like it's nothing. He crosses the street, returns, and continues on toward the school.

There's a round of shooting now. Shots against the City Hall. But it's not the ones on the corner doing the shooting. We don't move from our observation point.

10:15

More gas near the Judicial Police headquarters.

The drunk turns around at the corner by the school.

Three guerrilleros come running to the corner. They talk with the group that was already there. They disappear.

I watch the man at the City Hall, policeman in blue, on his stomach on the roof, under a satellite dish. He aims in the direction of the park. "There's more than one," says my sister Aura. "Look, there they are," and she passes me the binoculars. "They're crawling." Yes, I can see them, aiming at the park.

The war manifestos continue on the radio. By this time we've heard a justification for the armed uprising, a War Tax Law, and a series of petitions to international organizations like the Red Cross that ask for witnesses to the combat, and for help with the wounded and with burial of the dead. They've repeated the Declaration of War a few times and the instructions for the members of the EZLN, a series of rights and obligations of the people fighting in the "liberated zones," and a series of rights and obligations of the "soldiers of the EZLN." They speak of respect for the civilian population. They cite the Geneva Convention. There will be summary judgments for police and soldiers who've received foreign training, they are accused of betraying the country. Members of the EZLN who rob, kill, or violate civilians will be punished.

The revolutionary litany continues. The echo of words like "summary judgments," "executions," "combats," "war," "enemies of the revolution," "dead and wounded" produces an atmosphere of cold silence.

10:22

Another group on the corner. All very young, twenty or less. These look like university students: they all look completely *ladino*. One has a thin beard. The others, from before, were all clearly *indígenas*.

I can't see the men on the roof of City Hall anymore.

10:24

Yesterday and the day before, the rumors were flying: armed men were coming, "the Indios are going to occupy the town," "five Guatemalan airplanes came," "the Indios in Monte Líbano are ready now." Rumors.

"It's going to be the same as October 12, nothing will happen."

And joking toasts: "To the guerrilleros, who'll make heads roll tomorrow."

"Make heads roll" is a common refrain in these valleys where the machete is both tool and weapon; the most useful and the first one learns to wield. All of us, since childhood, had our own machete corresponding to our age, and we used them for everything: to slice *ocote*, to chop wood, to cut twigs for tiny corrals, to make toy bow and arrows, frames for kites, little horses from reeds, to cut and husk sugar cane. I look at the machetes that these guerrilleros are carrying: small, with holsters that look like *artesanía*, like toy machetes, all very uniform.

Make heads roll. Make heads roll. *Make heads roll.*

It doesn't sound the same as it did yesterday. As if the words have an edge now.

10:43

Four drunken young men go down the street now, with their bottle of Jaguar, an aguardiente made from sugar cane that's bottled in plastic liters and sells for about a dollar. They're part of a group of construction workers, "always ready to work hard and drink harder." "That one is Pato," says my sister Aura, an architect who knows them well. "The other is Caracol, the one with his shirt open." They walk along talking, stop, pass the bottle, say something. Unexpectedly, after taking a drink and passing the bottle, the one with his shirt open turns to the guerrillerros on the corner and shouts as loud as he can: "Assholes! Go ahead and kill me, you sons of bitches! You think we're afraid of you?" Pato wants to run up the street. The others hold him there. The armed ones ignore the shout.

These boys, without much encouragement, could join in the violence, on either side. They go on up the street, toward Don Amado's house, the old carpenter. (As children, when we used to hear hammering in the night, we knew that someone had died.) They talk, one lights a cigarette. They're really very drunk: New Year's. Three of them walk back down while one stays behind. "Come on, *cabrón.*"

We've been hearing sporadic shooting from the direction of the park; it's intensifying now. One of the drunken boys, as if responding to the shots, yells, "Ay, ay, ayyy . . . How life makes me laugh while I suffer!" They all light a cigarette.

I'm surprised by this, their almost animalistic posture of defiance that consists of baring the chest and swaggering as straight as they can. And they go on down the street, challenging anyone.

There's a strange tension burning in the air. Left by these young men who have no weapons but their bottle of Jaguar.

10:47

More gas from the park.

We try to call Mexico City, but get cut off. The rumor is flying that the lines have been intercepted by the guerrilla. Has it gotten that far?

Jaime, with his yellow baseball cap, passes by. He's the caretaker on the land where we're building my house, in the eastern part of town. It's a privileged spot, with a view of the valley. "Jaime's happy, thinking he's going to end up with your house," my sister Dora says, smiling.

The drunken boys pass by again, heading up the street. The group of guerrilleros on the corner haven't moved. Caracol knows he's being watched: the people in front of the store, the group up the street, and us, watching from the terrace. He resumes shouting at the soldiers on the corner: "Shoot me here!" and he pounds hard on his naked chest. The onlookers smile or laugh quietly. The curly-haired one is carrying the bottle now. They walk with more difficulty, continuing on up the street.

The guerrilleros have left the corner, or at least they aren't visible now. Another drunk appears, alone. Crosses the street. "Happy New Year!"

11:02

Carmelito is the owner of "El Cubanito," the store across the street. With the curtains drawn he's selling to the few who come, bringing fresh news.

They say that the guerrilleros have Don Enrique Solórzano tied up, along with his family.

"Poor Olga," says my mother, "what harm could Enrique have

13

done to them?" "How horrible of them!" says my Aunt Maga. "Didn't they say they would respect civilians?" adds Dora.

They took their things from the house and burned some of them. They've freed prisoners from the jail. They've already killed three Public Security police. They have the Solórzanos tied up, in their underwear. It looks like they're going to kill them.

11:12

On the radio, they're repeating the instructions for the Red Cross. Someone says it seems like we're in a movie. "Yeah, but it's awfully slow, we want more action," says Oswaldo, an eleven-year-old nephew.

11:29

Remarks in the store:

"We haven't heard a thing from the Federal Army."

"Wasn't there a detachment here?"

"We're so far from everything."

"It's an invasion."

"There's a lot of Central Americans."

"A lot of them don't speak."

"They look like Salvadoreños."

"No, they're like Guatemalans."

"They're Nicaraguans."

"But there are a lot of Indios from around here."

"From here?"

"Yes, the ones with the rubber boots are from around here, they were talking in Tzeltal!"

"Some are carrying wooden rifles."

"There are women."

"*We're so far from everything!*"

That's true.

11:36

A masked group passes by the corner, with guns. Mario said a while ago that there were a lot like these. They're the first I've seen with their faces covered. Ski masks or bandanas. A woman is with them. "Look how that one walks. It's a woman, look at the hair!" Yes . . . it looks like a woman.

11:40

The Mexican television presents the news. They don't say anything about the shooting, that it hasn't stopped in all this time. Minimal: a group of campesinos, armed with sticks, has occupied the City Hall of San Cristóbal. They don't know anything.

The sun is burning, in spite of the cloudy day. Bird song accompanies the sounds of shooting. A bullet goes whistling by, close. From where?

11:58

Two boys go by the corner, through the armed men. People adapt to anything. A kind of calm has fallen. Inside the houses that I can see with my binoculars, people are washing clothes, preparing food, sweeping floors.

I watch the group of armed men on the corner, near the school. Their bandanas are red stains against the white wall. Another group on Lety's corner. "Today we say, 'Enough!'" That's how the Declaration of War against the "dictator" begins. Sometimes the voice of the one who's reading changes. How many could there be?

Again I see the men in blue on the roof of City Hall. Two Zapatistas cross the street at the corner: one a girl with her face uncovered, the other masked.

12:32

We're on the terrace that looks onto the street: my sister Aura, my wife, my cousin Pablo, my brother-in-law Luis. We still see the group on the corner and the one by the school. Aura says: "Look . . . they've gotten up onto the roof of the school!"

"Where?"

"There, near that stack of tiles!"

The guerrillero commander is watching the ones in blue guarding the City Hall. From rooftop to rooftop. We can see the policemen in blue under the satellite dish.

"They have them on their stomachs."

"On their backs," someone says.

"They're aiming!"

"They're going to shoot!"

"No!"

"Yes!"

A shot sounds. The one in blue slumps down under the antenna. We're stunned. *Have we really seen this?* We've seen this so many times on television and now, before the actual fact, we're shaking. We look at each other, incredulous.

We're behind some walls under construction. When did we hide here? We had been on the terrace, openly watching the street. We wanted to shout when they aimed. "But if you shout, they'll shoot you, for sure." We took refuge in the part under construction, behind the terrace, unconsciously. From here I watch and write, protected by a wall.

The men in blue are moving quickly on the roof of City Hall. Looks like they're going down by some exit.

12:38

The commandos have the Judicial Police headquarters between two lines of fire now. We can see it from the door. The group on the roof on Lety's corner are shooting in order: the first in line takes the position on one knee, aims, shoots, and goes to the rear. The second does the same. That way, until they all do it. The ones on the roof of the school are doing the same.

"Those guys on the roof of the Judicial Police, some real little machos, aren't they?" says my father, trying to provoke something. "Let them come out and fight, instead of hiding in there! Or maybe now they remember when they beat Martín to death!"

(Martín came to Ocosingo when he was around nine years old. He ran away from his home, near Tenango, and earned his living in town as an errand boy, by shining shoes and selling gum. When the highway was built and the Lacandonia buses began to arrive, around 1971, Martín became a porter of heavy boxes and packages. One time, a crate of tomatoes fell on him, badly damaging his spine. He couldn't walk for a long while, and the people in town made him a little wagon which he used to get around, followed by a group of children, his workers, whom he commanded with surprising leadership ability. It would go like this: "We've got to get up this big hill, *cabrones*! Everybody ready to pull?" invited Martín. "Síííííí . . . !" shouts the band. "All right then, let's go, *cabrones* ! Some in front, and the rest in back! On three now, push, pull . . . !" And the wagon would rise quickly to the summit of the Avenida Central, in the midst of name-calling, swearing, shouts, and laughter. The children brought him food, did his errands, lit his cigarettes, went to buy his bottle.

Finally, he was able to walk again, but the lesion in his spinal column deformed him. From then on, the younger generations knew him as Martín the Hunchback. My own children, while still quite young, came upon him once on the street, completely drunk and dancing "*The Crazy Mosquito*."

On one of my visits to town I heard the news: for some problem, some robbery somewhere, the Judicial Police had detained Martín. They beat him so badly that they killed him. They dumped his body near the highway, covered in an old quilt.)

"Yes, but those were others . . . They got rid of them a while ago," says my mother.

"No, all of those damned *judiciales* are the same," my father says.

12:43

People get used to anything: the group of watchers has grown on the corner. They hide when the guerrilleros are shooting, and come out during the breaks.

What's this? When this round of shots finishes, three children appear, running to collect the shells. The same by the school: two kids are collecting the bullet casings, and seem to be having a great time.

13:00

A group of five arrives to join the guerrilleros on the corner: heavier weaponry. One with a ski mask. They shoot at the Judicial Police. You can hear the shattering of windows breaking after the shots. A lot of shooting, all of them now. Another round. Then they go. The original group stays. Again, the children after the shells. And the watchers. A long silence.

13:28

Calm. A great silence. Roosters crowing at midday. There are no motors, no radios, no noise. You can hear everything, like in the sweet past.

"This is something from old Samuel," says my aunt.

"It's a joke," says Luis.

"So many rats in the government, and they're everywhere, even in San Cristóbal," says my father.

A telephone call from San Cristóbal: the Federal Army is flying over the city. They're coming here. On the radio, the same song: "To advance onto the capital of the republic, conquering the Federal Army." And the rebel announcer enunciates every letter, defiant, sure, proud. The town is his. There are flashes of brilliance and ingenious moments in this discourse which is, at times, coarse.

I remember my sense of foreignness upon arriving in my marvelous valley in the last few years. Entering the town, finding graffiti like "Traitors to the Proletariat" on a wall of Pancho Vásquez's house. Or "Liberate Dr. Felipe Sorano." Or, simply, "PROCUP." "And this?" I asked myself, "What's going on here?" And asking and asking, one becomes drunk with a cocktail of acronyms: PROCUP, PDLP, GPP, CIOAC, OCEZ, ACIEZ, ANCIEZ, UNORCA, ARIC, CNC, and E-T-C. And all of them know a piece of our history.

There are, also, formal studies, some of long duration, about the organizations that work in the jungle. I remember a serious study about Las Cañadas which ICIIC, a state agency, published a few years ago. It talks about the catechists of liberation theology, and their diligent work to install "the reign of God" in Lacandonia. It talks of PROCUP and its line of Prolonged Popular War. It tells of the Party of the Poor.

The townspeople still remember the engineer Cardel, who lived in Ocosingo many years and was detained with the FALN (Armed Forces of National Liberation), who had a training camp in El Diamante. It's common knowledge that groups with Maoist tendencies, like Popular Politics, Proletarian Line, Line of the Masses, and Leading Idealogic Line have been here for twenty years. From these sprang ARIC — Union of Unions — and UNORCA.

Pilla, my wife, explains to me that Popular Politics split into Line of the Masses and Proletarian Line, for who knows what reasons in its leadership, when they were working in the north. "The OID have the same roots, although I don't remember what was the problem with them. The ones from Line of Masses were there in Teléfonos, when Josie and I arrived to work with the women," adds my wife, remembering the Glorious Times.

Finally, everybody knows that the political activists and the catechists work together. "If they're not the same, they have something to do with each other."

"Each to his own, but all together," says my brother, Rodulfo.

14:00

News on the television: "24 Hours." They totally diminish the size of the problem — or else they don't know. Nothing about the Declaration of War. They talk about a group of armed Indians. They refer to San Cristóbal. A call comes in to give more precise information, but it's about San Cristóbal. They don't know anything about what's happening here in Ocosingo.

14:25

A man passes by on a motorcycle, coming from the park. He seems to get along well with the guerrilleros, though he's dressed in a T-shirt and shorts. He passes calmly through the armed group at the school. He stops his bike and yells: "Set fire to that fucking thing, *compadre* ! The gasoline's already there!" And he laughs. He's referring to a truck, parked in front of the Judicial Police, on the sidewalk of Dora Cashcarita's house. He rides up our street.

"He lives here, up there, and he's been helping them since this morning," they comment in the store.

"Isn't that Eleuterio's son?"

"They say his wife's a Salvadoreña whom he brought from the jungle."

"Oh God, Ocosingo's full of Salvadoreños . . . especially in that neighborhood up there."

14:40

Paca, another niece, comes running into the dining room. "Uncle, they've set fire to the truck." I race out.

Flames under the truck. Explosion: the tires. The fire grows. Dense black smoke. There are people moving inside the house. They come out into the hallway of the second floor. They're screaming, terrified: women and children. I see them go down-stairs, running, but inside the house. They disappear. They reappear now, and begin to pass small children through a hedge, next to my cousin Toño's house. Shouts for help. Some of the people watching on the corner run to help. The armed ones are impassive. The house could burn down, the flames are mounting so much. If the car explodes, the house will definitely burn. The watchers grab the small children through the hedge. The women and men jump. More shouts. The last woman gets out. They run up the sidewalk toward Don Beto Ruiz's house, here on the corner.

No effort to stop the fire. There's nothing to be done. There isn't a fire department in the town. No water, either. (That's been the biggest problem since the day before yesterday: a town surrounded by water, with three rivers flowing through it, has no water because the municipal administration changed the person in charge; and the new person, a civil engineer who "that's the last straw, he's not even from here," did something to make the valves burst and ruined the hydraulic system. Right in the middle of the holidays. The mayor "was in Tuxtla" and couldn't be reached, for some reason.)

The group of watchers up above has grown to around a hundred people. On the corner down below, my Uncle José is yelling, "Let's do something! We're defenseless! We can't just stand here watching!" And we all want to do something. But don't know what. Anyway we have no water to put out the fire. Nor has the decision been made to pass through the guerrilleros and stop what they've started and are now watching burn, smiling.

14:58

Pancho and Marco, Toño's sons, come to ask us to keep their truck here. "In case the fire spreads."

15:05

I open the door. I watch Toño back out his truck and drive up here. He comes in. We talk.

Last night, at one in the morning, we went to give them the New Year's embrace, as is our custom. Always, after the late-night supper, either they come here, or we go there. Before, we would have the feast together: Aunt Flor's family and my mother's (they're sisters). Now our families have each grown so large that we don't celebrate together, except for the embrace. Last night we did it at about one in the morning. The town was already being invaded. We didn't know anything was happening.

15:15

Mirrors explode in the house on fire.

15:22

More shots. The flames in the truck diminish. It looks like the house will be saved, despite the blackened walls. The shooting continues.

Toño tells me that they took Chibeto from his house, along with his whole family. They needed the house as an observation point. They didn't bother them much. Now they're in his sister-in-law Estela's house.

More shots. More tear gas. From the terrace inside the house you can see the spouts of smoke after the shots. The guerrilleros are shooting at the City Hall, and they are responding with gas.

15:41

Movement in the upper floors of City Hall. Shouting. White flags waving a sign of peace. A lot of white flags.

15:43

The shouting grows. The Public Security Forces have surrendered. Everyone comes out to look. The shout sets fire to the streets: "They've surrendered! They've given up! And now?" You can hear an intense clamor spreading throughout the town. The defeated police should be leaving now, and the rebels: victorious.

15:57

The guerrilleros are running down there from the school now, protecting themselves in doorways and covering each other, military-style.

The radio from Villahermosa says that five hundred soldiers are coming from Palenque.

I go out the door. Many people have come out onto the corner, cautiously. They risk a bit more. They go down now, two or three meters, looking toward the park. A compact little mountain of watchers. Someone arrives from behind, vigilant. All of a sudden he shouts, "PUM!" Everyone jumps; the first smiles in a long time. The crowd is growing by the minute. I go on, to the corner.

Rumors: they dynamited the bridge over La Florida (the river that comes from San Cristóbal) and the one over La Vírgen (from Palenque). I don't believe it. We would have heard the explosions. Especially the last one: it's very close. They burned down the City Hall in San Cristóbal. They burned down the *Ganadera* here. But we didn't see the smoke.

16:13

Three men on the corner. Uniforms. Small machetes. Red scarves. Another group uses machetes and rifle butts to break open the door of the Judicial Police. The ones on the corner cover them. There, near the ones busting open the door, there's a good-size group of watchers.

16:18

They open up the offices and find a man. They take out some things and review the room and patio. Apparently the comandante remained there, alone. The rest of the *judiciales* had already escaped since morning. A group of guerrilleros take the man in the white shirt towards the park.

16:21

A sheep bleats among the multitudes that have come to look into the offices of the Judicial Police or to count the bullet holes in the doors and walls. The sheep walks on, bleating, to the corner — the image of confusion and abandonment. That's how many of us feel now: a confused flock.

16:37

The radio: "Attention, people of Mexico. In these moments Radio Zapata informs: we have just learned that the Public Security Forces of this town have surrendered to the forces of the EZLN."

16:58

Rumor on the corner: "They killed the comandante."
"He had already surrendered, even had his hands in the air."
"A woman did it, right there in the doorway."
"Surrendered or not, they shot him in the head! And left him right there, in the doorway of the City Hall."

17:03

Dora and Génner are going down to the park. Rodulfo and my wife are going, too.

17:05

Mario and Ovidio return. More news: they have hostages in the *Ganadera*. Don Enrique, Luis Pascasio, Dr. Talango, Rolando Pascasio and another of Don Enrique's sons-in-law. They have them tied up, with their hands behind their backs, in their underwear.

17:33

My wife comes back, very affected. Dead bodies in pools of blood. Red handprints on the columns of City Hall. They've got forty police tied up, shirtless, on the floor. "Tied up with their hands behind their backs. There they are, with faces full of surprise and fear." And with these they're going to negotiate the fall of Salinas.

I look out at the beautiful late afternoon: blue sky, thick white clouds over the mountains to the east, an orange sun. A call comes in from Tijuana: it's my mother-in-law. They already know the news in the United States. Calls come in, but we can't call out.

17:44

"The Mexican Alarm Clock" is the organ of communication of the EZLN. They say on Radio Zapata that their recent edition published the Declaration of War on the government and the federal army.

There's no water in the town.

The thick white clouds are growing over the mountains.

18:00

Radio Zapata broadcasts a song in verse, accompanied by percussion. Quite talented in general, although the refrain is bad. The rest is entertaining. The verses broadcast nothing less than a formula to make explosives!

18:10

My brother Rodulfo is going to sleep at his house. He and Conchita, his wife, have been here all day. My mother doesn't want them to go, but Rodulfo insists. I remember now that Mario said that the rebels made trenches in the road to make it impassable, and that there were guerrilleros posted along the road to stop anyone falling into them. "There are men in the hills, hidden in the tall grass."

It's cold. Night has fallen. The lights have come on. A group of six guerrilleros have been on guard on the corner all afternoon. There are similar guards on all the corners.

On the radio they say that they will not permit the EZLN to be disparaged as a group of narco-traffickers, a narco-guerrilla, or a group of bandits.

I feel tired. I've hardly eaten, but I'm not hungry. I've not stopped writing.

We wanted news, but the only thing on TV is "Don Francisco" on one channel and American football on the other. "I hope that the Zapatistas liberate us from this pigsty," I say to my wife. "And what if instead of that they play José de Molina?" she responds, and I remain quiet.

I listen to the radio where I hear, for the millionth time, that the flag of the rebels is black and red. They give the call to unite with the armed struggle. Ask the Congress to depose the "dictator." Invite donations to continue their initiative to advance on the capital of the republic. They will permit the people in the "liberated zones" to freely elect their administrative authorities. They will respect the lives of their prisoners. There will be summary judgments and executions of members of the police or the army who have received foreign training or help: they are accused, from this moment, of betraying the country. But they will respect those who surrender. They will ask for the surrender of the enemy army before each combat.

20:15

Talking in the dining room:

Aunt Maga: "And where's that nasty bishop gotten to now? . . ."

Me: "I don't think he has anything to do with it: the church says it doesn't approve of armed struggle for change, that it rejects violence. If the bishop wasn't here, the uprising would have happened a long time ago."

Dora: "Well, you and the bishop can say Mass, but . . ."

20:20

My children call from Mexico City. We explain the situation to them and try to calm them as much as possible. We ask them to keep calling at this hour every day.

20:34

A shot.

21:15

A call from Mexico City, Josie. She tells us that Radio Mil was giving information and interviewing people. Talking about some leader speaking in English with the tourists in San Cristóbal. Affirms that it seems to be a coordinated operation of large dimensions, that she and Edgar have been analyzing the information, but still can't figure out where it's all coming from.

21:57

I've had a headache all day. I think since the first tear gas explosion.

22:22

Josie is calling again: Patrocinio González is already in Chiapas. They interviewed guerrilleros in San Cristóbal: they want the president and the entire cabinet to resign.

Channel 2 is showing "The Best of 1993." A little while ago, "Candid Camera." While tension smothers the town, national television transmits this trash. We feel so isolated. Defenseless. A phrase comes to me from this morning: *we're so far from everything.*

23:35

Images from San Cristóbal on the news: declarations from the federal and state governments. They interview two guerrilleros. Everything looks different there: no Central Americans, no one leading the others, no violence, no hostages, no attacks on civilians, no dead. And the guerrilleros being interviewed are clearly *indígenas*. Because of the tourism and the press in San Cristóbal? Image control? But "24 Hours" hides the Declaration of War. They're passing it all off as some indigenous or campesino demands of minor importance. The government is offering dialogue, affirming that the army will not intervene. The images show the access to the town blocked by enormous felled trees. The news ends.

Uneasiness: everything seems so strange. I go out onto the roof looking over the street, the part under construction. The rebels guarding the intersection are asleep in a ball on the sidewalk. I think I see one sitting in the doorway of Don Beto Ruiz's house.

I make this last note at 2:39. It's already another day. My wife is waiting for me in the warm bed.

A thought accompanies me: reality always has its reason. Whatever happens.

EK

SEEDS OF A REVOLT

Alberto Huerta

SITTING FOR SEVERAL WEEKS IN THE TOWN SQUARE of San Cristóbal de las Casas late in the summer of 1993, I was struck by the number of police and military personnel circling the *zócalo*. When the Maya — young Ch'oles, Tzotziles, and Tzeltales — came into town, they seemed almost imperceptible, except for their colorful tribal clothing. The Indios from San Juan Chamula, in white-and-black ponchos, and the Tzeltales in red ponchos with a rising sun motif, broke the pattern of uniformed soldiers standing about everywhere. I sat alone and read at the same park bench every afternoon, while the police circled the *zócalo* and the Maya went about like clockwork figures selling their native wares. By 5 P.M., the Indios had returned to their villages, leaving the plaza nearly empty.

One afternoon, boredom encouraged some of the Indios to ask what I was reading. The book I held in my hands was by Rosario Castellanos, author of *Balún Canán* and *Oficio de tinieblas*, novels about San Cristóbal and the plight of the indigenous peoples. Most did not know about Mexico's first woman ambassador, who was born and reared in Comitán de Domínguez, Chiapas, and who died in middle age. I told them she had directed my work at the Universidad Iberoamericana in Mexico City, when I was young like them. They laughed and then became somber.

One, José, asked if I knew about Comitán. Way back in 1940, a president had promised the Indios there a piece of land *(un paraje)* for each Indio. But three years ago, the promise had been erased when their land was forcibly taken by the Mexican Army. A minor rebellion had taken place and a group known as the Organización Campesina Emiliano Zapata [Emiliano Zapata Farmworkers' Organization] was formed. They asked if I knew of the hero of the 1910 Mexican Revolution, Emiliano Zapata, and I nodded. Another said OCEZ was a group that was seeking to redress disputes over land titles. One even said that open rebellion might take place before December. It was my turn to laugh. How could an uprising take place with so great a police presence in San Cristóbal? Their expressions became opaque. No one spoke for a while.

Then another asked if I knew that the President of Mexico had changed the Constitution. Miguel stated rhetorically: "How can the Constitution be changed after so many years?" I played devil's advocate and asked, "What changes?" Did I not know that Article 27 had changed their lives? Before, their *paraje* could not be sold. The dismantling of Article 27 had privatized all lands. They could sell now, and would probably be forced to sell by local landowners or the Mexican army. Miguel added: "Already we hear that the Japanese want a part of the Chiapas highlands for timber."

I responded in astonishment, "Here, so far away?"

They responded in unison, "Yes, here near the village of San Juan Chamula, where the Maya believe the creation was born." My friends eventually left and I continued reading.

When the armed occupation of San Cristóbal, Altamirano, Las Margaritas, Rancho Nuevo, and Ocosingo took place on New Year's day, I immediately called San Cristóbal to see if my friends were safe. My contact could tell me little, except that what had happened seemed inevitable: "The Maya know they will die in shame when government forces come to take posssession of their *paraje*, so some feel they might as well die with dignity, defending what little they have." It is winter and I do not laugh now.

CHIAPAS IS AN EXTREMELY POOR STATE. EIGHTY percent of its municipalities are in a state of neglect classified by the Mexican government as "acute marginalization." Data for 1990 from the National Population Council show that out of a population of over 3.5 million, 30.1 percent are illiterate, while 62 percent did not complete their primary education. Almost a quarter of the population (885,605) are Ch'ol, Lacandón, Tzeltal, Tzotzil, Tojolabal, and Zoque Indians. More than 35 percent of the state's dwellings lack electricity or drainage, while 51 percent have earthen floors and 70 percent are overcrowded. Nineteen percent of the working population receives no income and nearly 40 percent receives less than the daily minimum wage [11 pesos, roughly $3.00 per day], while 21.2 percent receives between one and two minimum wages. Sixty-five percent of the population is scattered among communities with fewer than 5,000 inhabitants.

The situation is even worse in the Los Altos and jungle regions, where the armed uprising began. Forty-nine percent of the nearly half a million inhabitants of the area, mostly mono-lingual Indians, are illiterate, while more than 70 percent of the population over fifteen did not finish primary school. Eighty percent of all dwellings are overcrowded, have earthen floors, and no drainage or sanitary services. Only one out of every ten people has a daily income of more than two minimum wages [22 pesos, $6.00] (*El Financiero*, January 5, 1994).

Paradoxically, Chiapas possesses natural resources that are strategically important for the country. It is Mexico's largest generator of hydroelectric energy, with its four reservoirs accounting for 55 percent of the country's total production. By contrast, in 1990, 30 percent of all dwellings had no electricity, 40 percent lacked piped water, and only 2.9 percent of agricultural land had irrigation systems. As for gas and oil production, Chiapas has been the country's third- and fourth-largest producer, respectively, for a decade. It also possesses abundant natural resources, some of them under-used, such as its 156-mile coastline, and others over-exploited, risking ecological catastrophe, such as the Lacandón jungle, whose rate of destruction is so rapid that in the past thirty years it has lost 70 percent of its resources (María del Carmen Legorreta Gómez, *La república, de Aguascalientes a Zacatecas*).

Health services are insufficient and ineffective. Poverty-related diseases, preventible through vaccination and sanitary measures — such as intestinal and respiratory infections, tuberculosis, malaria, and river blindness — are the main causes of illness and death.

*Paulina Hermosillo, Hortensia Sierra, and
Elizabeth Luis Díaz*

DON JORGE IS SIXTY YEARS OLD, A TOJOLABAL FROM
the community of Guadalupe Tepeyac:

"Our ancestors could barely live on the lands they were given.
Well, for that matter, they distributed very little. As the years
passed, this land was divided among our grandfathers, fathers,
uncles, and cousins, and our share of a piece of land has been
getting smaller and smaller. Also, when the land was first distributed, what you got many times was limestone, and you
couldn't farm because the land was sterile. And if we keep dividing when we inherit, each time the piece is smaller. We don't have
a place to harvest, to live. Because we're born on the earth, we
eat, and we die."

María is twenty-two years old, a Tzeltal. She lives in a small house, made of mud and reeds. She was our hostess, and shared what she had. In gratitude, all of us gave her some money. Her husband killed a pig to offer us meat — something people only do on very special occasions. Urban visitors are not able to comprehend how they can eat the same thing all their lives. For instance, someone from Human Rights asked, "What is a typical dish?" Coffee, beans, and tortillas are the basis of their nourishment.

"I was born a Catholic. Have you seen the church of the Virgin of Guadalupe?

"I'd like to know, where is Chiapas on a map? And where do you live? Where is the sea? Are there as many plants in other places as there are here?

"I only know how to make baskets and clay *comales*. I learned Spanish in the EZLN. I was in it for four years, and I met my husband in the Zapatista Army. He doesn't speak Spanish, and that's why he's embarrassed to be present when you're here. I had to leave the army because I was going to have a baby.

"Our struggle is not for money, but for good land to live on and fair prices for our harvests."

María's mother is a woman in her forties, which we had to calculate, since she doesn't remember her age. This woman (also named María) also lives in a mud hut, with eleven children. Her eldest, María, is already married; her youngest is a baby girl of three months, whom she breast-feeds when she has milk, and when she doesn't, she gives her coffee.

"My daughter has no name yet, but she'll be called Hortensia. It's a pretty name. She's sick and I don't have any medicine to give her. I want to baptize her, just in case something happens."

María is a woman with a very strong will and a conviction to change the future for her children. She is very interested to know what people think after January 1st. Proudly, she asks, "What do you think of us? What do you think of the Zapatista Army?"

Isidora is twenty years old, a Tzeltal:

"There were already rumors that an army was being organized in the mountains, and I found out that there were women in this army. That gave me the courage to escape, because I wanted to be free, free as all the compañeros who lived there in that army. I wanted to learn what they knew — to read and write. Well, in my community, although there's a school, there are no teachers, and there is nothing else to do than carry wood and help in the kitchen.

"At thirteen I went to join them, but since I was so young and I had left without my parents' or the community's permission, they   the Zapatistas — returned me to my home, where I was punished and they beat me for having left. That was the custom.

"I left again to join the army, and was returned, but I was determined and went to look for them again. I spoke with Subcomandante Marcos and told him that if they didn't accept me, I would not rest until I was in the army, or else I'd die of the beatings from my uncle. Seeing how determined I was, the Committee had a meeting with my community, because they didn't want to have problems or have people saying that they were robbing young girls from the communities. And in this council they asked the community's authorization, since the indigenous tradition obliges the women to be dedicated to her home and to serve her husband. But my conviction was stronger, and everyone accepted my decision."

Captain Irma, a Ch'ol, is twenty-two years old:

"I fight because we have nothing, neither land, schools, nor hospitals. The land isn't sufficient for the crops. We need training to work at other jobs, since if we're not trained well, what are we going to live from, without land?

"The situation is difficult. There have been various organizations and changes of government who promise that now, really, this time they'll keep their promises. I think there's no faith in the government, and I don't see any answers in their actions. The government can say that it has kept all its promises, that it has helped, but those are only words."

Lieutenant Elena is in the Medical Corps. She is a Tzeltal, eighteen years old:

"How old am I? I'm ancient.

"People in my family have died for lack of medicine. It was poverty which made me join the Zapatista Army. We used to harvest coffee, but they won't pay us what it's worth. And then if we want to transport our harvest, we have no road, and it's very hard to carry the load. My younger brother died not long ago — we can't get the ill past the military checkpoints.

"Every day there's work to do, there are sick compañeros who need to be examined. In the mornings we do training exercises, and we know what the injuries look like. Right now, the only medicine we have is antibiotics. Our job is to prevent malaria.

"It was a wounded compañera who took command and ordered us to fire back at the enemy when the officer in command was paralyzed by so many bullets falling around him. He just didn't know what to do. The compañera organized the defense of our positions and we were in combat all that day.

"Everything that I've learned has been while in the Zapatista Army."

Captain Martín is a Tzeltal, eighteen years old:

"I'm eighteen years old and have been in the Zapatista Army for three years. When I was a boy, I studied whenever a teacher would come, but I didn't like it because I felt they didn't teach me well. I never had anything when I was young, and when I grew up I realized I could join the armed organization. I joined and learned to use weapons and to speak Spanish.

"Many women have joined the Zapatista Army and to me it makes no difference if it's a woman who takes command. Here we're all equal, men and women. I have three brothers and three sisters, and they're all in the Zapatista Army, and have been for seven years.

"The government thinks we're a bunch of bandits and that they'll finish with us soon. On the contrary, we're going to beat them because we consciously know why we are fighting. I don't think the government is going to accomplish what it says. They're sending airplanes to observe us; they want to know so they can screw us. We're not going to give up our weapons. We're going to keep on being soldiers forever, to defend the people and to make it possible for them to take public offices. We do what the people say; the people rule. If we live, so much the better, but if we die, it's to defend the people.

AM

VOICES FROM THE MASKS
Blanche Petrich

ALBERTO, THE ONLY MAN IN HIS TOWN WHO MAKES pottery — in Ahuatenango, working with clay is considered a woman's job — was up before the sun on the first day of the year. He had an errand to run in Teopisca, after which he planned to take a bus to San Cristóbal de las Casas to celebrate the New Year with his friends. But at the bus stop he ran into an acquaintance.

"Where you headed?"

"San Cristóbal."

"Don't go. It's full of guerrilleros."

"Go on, what war?"

"Well, the Third World War."

Ramona

In the Chiapas highlands, on the sides of roads that are almost always laced with fog, the campesino families walk: the head of the family in the lead, his wife following, holding a few chickens by their feet, a bundle of firewood on her back, a child strapped onto her chest, and several more clinging to her skirt.

If there's a pair of shoes for the family, they'll belong to the man. If there aren't enough tortillas to go around, it will be the woman who does without. He might speak Spanish. She is undoubtedly monolingual. As will be her daughters, destined to be tiny mothers to their own brothers, and who from their first steps will learn to always walk behind the men, in silence, with their heads down.

But on that Tuesday when the leaders of the Clandestine Revolutionary Indigenous Committee (CCRI) of the Zapatista National Liberation Army (EZLN) appeared for the first time before a group of strangers to explain the reasons for their armed uprising, Comandante Ramona, the only woman in the group, did not walk behind the men, but came in at their side.

Nor did she come with her head down, but held high, looking directly at us, and as openly curious as we were, looking at her.

The CCRI — the EZLN's general command — is a civilian leadership, elected democratically in popular assemblies as representives of the Zapatista communities. Hierarchically, it has authority over the EZLN's military command. Each region and each ethnic group has its own CCRI.

Like the others, Ramona carried her weapon slung across her chest — it was an old and well-oiled rifle. And like the rest, she had things she wanted to say. But her desire to speak and my desire to interview her crashed against a language barrier. (I don't speak Tzotzil.) Some of what she said made it across, with the help of a mangled translation by a young EZLN guerrillera. But Ramona had a lot to say and she was in a hurry, and so she didn't make the necessary pauses for her interpreter. She understood my questions. And each of her answers began, "Well, you see . . ."

Before becoming a comandante of the CCRI, Ramona was an embroiderer. The *huipiles* from her home town, San Andrés Larrainzar, are among the finest, richest, and most elaborate in the Mayan world. Each piece would take about three years to finish, and then she would go down to San Cristóbal to sell it to one of the handicraft shops. She was paid mere crumbs for her works of art.

Ramona talked about the Tzotzil women, how they are the first to rise, long before dawn, and the last to collapse onto a mat at night. "A lot of suffering," she says. In her speech in Tzotzil, she stresses the word "exploitation."

She recounts the poverty of her people, how they don't have enough to feed their children and how the land refuses to yield food. She says she has no children, that she chose to carry a rifle instead. She says the objective of her struggle is to free her people from injustice, to achieve freedom and the points enumerated in the EZLN's Declaration of War. In Spanish, she repeats, "Democracy. Freedom. Justice."

Her head of black hair is already beginning to show a few strands of grey.

Within the EZLN structure, Ramona and the rest of the members of the CCRI from her region are leaders with more power than that of Subcomandante "Marcos." Marcos receives his orders from them. Ramona managed to win the respect and authority she now holds by, in her own words, "daring to speak out in the Assembly," and to actively participate in the organization.

Ramona said many things that day, but I couldn't understand what she said in Tzotzil. She concluded by inviting all Mexican women to follow the example of the Zapatistas.

Ramona was dressed in traditional clothes, but when she spoke officially as a comandante she put on a man's sweater and hid her face with a bandana. Her tiny boots peeked out from under the muddied hem of her skirt.

Days later, Ramona became a legend. During the negotiations in the cathedral, due to her high rank, she always appeared directly to the left of the mediator, Samuel Ruiz, bishop of San Cristóbal de las Casas. She wore a ski mask and her brilliant San Andrés *huipil*. She never spoke, but her silence was strident, punctuated by the flickering of her black eyes. Because of her small stature, a journalist named her *"llaverito"* [little key chain]. When she sat at the negotiations table, her feet didn't reach the ground.

After that event, she has never again appeared in public.

New Year

The war scenario we always imagined taking place in Central American countries but never, never in Mexico, erupted suddenly, with a roar, on New Year's Day 1994, the smell of gunpowder everywhere, and the press photographing the bloody corpses for posterity, to dispel any doubts.

Defeated or compromised, the guerrilla warfare which had characterized Latin America in the 1970s and 1980s had faded away into the horizon. Mexico, classified at the international level as a "middle power," the modest associate of the United States, was expected to cast off its Third World status once and for all in 1994 when it entered its first year of the North American Free Trade Agreement. Who in their right mind would venture speculation that Mexico would experience a new armed struggle? No one.

The International Year of Indigenous People was ending, without having managed to move Native people from their corner of neglect, despite the efforts of Nobel Prize – winner

44

Rigoberta Menchú. The poverty of forty million Mexicans was not on anyone's agenda. If by chance the government happened to mention their extreme poverty, it was solely in the context of its National Solidarity Program, the pampered brainchild of the Salinas administration. Poverty was an abstract concept, nothing more.

After the Zapatista uprising, people liked to imagine how the Mexican ruling class toasted the New Year: happy, self-congratulatory, satisfied — until just a few hours after midnight, when the traditional glass of champagne had barely been drained, the civilized world received a phone call with the alarming news from the extreme south of Mexico. A general was surrounded by rebels in his new, modern barracks. The headquarters of the Rancho Nuevo military zone, built atop a pantheon of Tzeltal deities, was also under attack by irregular troops. And that wasn't the worst of it. The proud colonial city of San Cristóbal de las Casas had been seized by several columns of armed men and women. A group had occupied the City Hall. They had blocked the roads.

They called themselves the Zapatista National Liberation Army. And there was more. More? Yes. Ocosingo and Las Margaritas were also occupied by guerrilla fighters. As much as a third of the entire state of Chiapas had been blockaded by the rebels. Not even the Salvadoran FMLN, the most capable and best-organized guerrilla army in modern history, had dreamed of an insurgent operation of this caliber.

The armed confrontations lasted eleven days, claiming many lives and displacing thousands of people. The government conducted air raids on populated areas and villages — a scandal reported in the international press. It waged psychological war against the Zapatistas, a dirty war of disinformation. The Mexican army mobilized artillery and aviation forces never seen before. At one point, thirteen generals of the federal army were convened in the 31st Military Zone of Rancho Nuevo in an attempt to resolve the worst national security crisis in Mexican history.

Among the general population, after the first moments of shock and fear subsided, there was an unstoppable surge of sympathy and understanding for the uprising of the Native people. "Why wouldn't they rebel!" people were saying. "This country has been extremely unfair to them." And while that was being said down below on the street, up above in the echelons of power, there was chaos. There were moments so critical that anarchy was feared: a power void, the absence of governing institutions.

Later came the truce and the word "negotiations."

And then everyone asked themselves who were those masked people, those Mayan insurrectionists, those end-of-the-millennium Zapatistas who had raised the flag of the Revolution that had begun the century in the name of Emiliano Zapata.

Sunday and the President

During the first week of the war, uncertainty and rage reigned in the top levels of the government. Although he later appeared otherwise, President Carlos Salinas de Gortari was convinced, and expressed it publicly, that the rebels were indigenous people who were being "manipulated" by outside interests.

At that time we went to consult the opinion of a Chamula named Mingo López, one of the sharpest analysts and experts on the subject. He is the leader of thousands of evangelical Indians who were expelled by the *caciques* of San Juan Chamula. He lives in a neighborhood called La Hormiga, on the outskirts of San Cristóbal, a community built by the exiled Indians with very little help from officials. The preceding year he had been imprisoned for nearly seven months in the Cerro Hueco jail, "accused" of agitation and of supporting Cuauhtémoc Cárdenas.

On the wall of his house, amid calendar pages, hang two full-color photographs of Mingo, completely decked out in full Chamula ceremonial dress, accompanied by Salinas, who is also dressed like a Chamula. One photograph was taken while Salinas was still a candidate; in the other he is the president.

"No," says Mingo, "the president is wrong. The Indian isn't some kind of bicycle, something to be ridden."

"Yes, but Mingo, how can you criticize the president? What do those photos mean, then?"

"Ah well, he came here to make promises. And I have these photos here so I don't forget the promises he hasn't kept."

Displaced

In the county seat of Las Margaritas, next to City Hall, is the Casa Ejidal. It has been turned into a refuge for the hundreds of families who abandoned their lands in the Altamirano gorge in fear of the war. The peasant organizations affiliated with the PRI and the "armies" — as the soldiers are called here — told the population that the Zapatistas were going to attack, that they were going to come and seize everything, and force the men to take up arms with them. "And that's how they coerced us to leave." It was the power of rumor which erased entire villages and hamlets.

Abelardo and his wife, Matilde, both Tzeltales, had just arrived from their *ejido*, Plan de Aguaprieta. A two-day journey on foot. Matilde complained:

"My feet are swollen from walking over the rocks. And I had to carry two children, one on my back. We left the coffee harvest behind, my little crop of corn, too. The gorge was deserted. Not a single soul stayed behind."

Everybody had reasons for fleeing:

"The army said that the Zapatistas were going to come."

"And that's why you left?"

"Yes. They say they're coming to rob us. Everything's fallen apart. We're nervous."

On the back wall of the Casa Ejidal there are two portraits: an oil painting and a photograph of Emiliano Zapata. And his life-size, full-body image prevails in a mural on another wall. The eyes of the displaced peasants look upon the icons, and they fall quiet.

A boy speaks up: "It's Emiliano Zapata. Is he with us, or not?"

The father of the family scratches his head. "The thing is so complicated. It's the party of Emiliano Zapata that has us on the run. Now they're saying that they're not after land, but concrete results."

There they stood, scratching their heads in doubt.

An Appointment

The leaders of the EZLN had secretly asked us to a meeting at the end of January, to express their point of view and respond to the thousands of questions that were swirling around them. It took place on February 1.

The winter of 1994 was harsh, and the hail that fell in the early mornings had destroyed the vegetables in photographer Antonio Turok's garden. He was my host while the final details of the interview to which we had been summoned were being finalized. Other colleagues had also been invited, including Elio Henríquez, Epigmenio Ibarra, and Philipe de Saint. Each morning, discouraged and without much to do, we'd go out and look at the lettuce leaves that had been burned by the cold; we were anxious to leave for the mysterious Zapatista territory and depressed as we sensed another day's wait ahead of us.

One day the signal finally came and we departed. Along the way we met up with the rest of the group. It's always the same; no matter how much one plans for a trip, in the end some important detail is always forgotten. We stopped to buy socks for Elio in one town. And it had never occurred to me that I'd need more than my light woven jacket. The excellent rain ponchos Epigmenio had managed to get for all of us were left behind there, forgotten. And, excited as we were, we made the serious mistake of eating something while we had the chance.

Finally, after a delay of two hours which seemed like twenty, our "connection" appeared, a stranger who smiled like a lifelong friend, and who had an iron hand for managing the capricious behavior often characteristic of journalists.

I never knew where it was we went. After many hours on the road, during which we received orders to "sleep" and not open our eyes, we arrived at the rebels' domain. The bus stopped on a dirt path and the guide calmly lit up a cigarette. The rest of us also quieted down.

A young man passed by, walking slowly. "Good afternoon," he said, smiling as he departed. A few steps farther on, he turned around. "Good afternoon," he repeated, on his way back. A few minutes later another young man appeared, but taller and older. "Good afternoon. How can I help you?" he asked politely, leaning up against the bus. At that point the guide extended his hand and read the password he carried jotted down on a small piece of paper. It was a poem:

> There is but one face and one thought within us.
> Our words walk with truth.
> In life and in death we will continue walking.
> There is no longer pain in death;
> there is hope in life.
> Choose.

The young man in the road also read a little note that he had in the palm of his hand. "It's OK," he said. "You're going to wait."

We would hear "you're going to wait" many times during our journey. After a moment stranded in the fog and silence, they had us go inside a small house made of boards with a dirt floor.

Many hours passed. In the darkness we suddenly noticed the heads of curious little children peeking in at us. The next apparitions were the Zapatistas, well-armed and in uniform.

They insisted upon seeing our credentials several times and inspected our boots in a military fashion, to see if they were suitable for the journey. We were intrigued when we had to hand over our watches. They illuminated our faces with their lanterns to better identify us. They issued orders with a rare mixture of Indian courtesy and military authority. We made part of the journey aboard a cargo truck covered with a canvas cloth. Even under the tarp we were told to close our eyes during certain stretches.

We passed through "customs" inside a hermitage. The little chapel was decorated for a party, the floor covered with *juncia*, or pine needles, as is the custom in that region. There were candles lit for the saints. A boy and a girl, both well-armed, guarded the door like two stone statues. We had a long wait, though it was livened up with talk about the latest developments. "They're taking the mines out of our path," they explained to us.

We made another stretch of the journey on horseback. Getting out of the truck at a predetermined spot, a column of masked guerrilleros and their cavalry awaited us. The moon was full. It surprised me to see that many of the masked militiamen were wearing skirts. These were militiawomen.

Captain Pedro was obviously concerned about the inconvenience of bringing a woman like me along with the group. In his native language, Tzotzil, he gave repeated advice to the rebel who was to guide the horse assigned to me. "It's the best horse we have, so don't worry, Miss," Pedro assured me. But then my guide took off at full speed. Pedro's yelling stopped him but the young man only responded to his reprimands with "Yes, captain, yes, captain." Finally someone explained, "He only speaks Ch'ol."

The idyllic journey by moonlight came to a sudden end when it began to rain and we realized that the plastic rain ponchos had been left behind in the truck. Soon, besides the cold rain, another storm had begun. Among the few Mayan words that the rebels spoke, I could distinguish one which they began to utter more frequently, "*Paliacate, paliacate* [bandana]." The moment had come to blindfold us.

Blindly we crossed streams and farmlands, climbing and descending, rain pouring over the bandanas. Without knowing how to ride a horse, straddling it awkwardly in and out of steep ravines, completely drenched, is rather, shall we say, distressing. Captain Pedro squeezed my hand. "You won't fall, Miss."

We arrived at dawn. Once again, the credentials. A woman without a ski mask approached me, offering a jug of water and her arm, since my legs were giving out. It was Major Ana María, the leader of the operation that had taken the City Hall of San Cristóbal. She offered us a place to sleep. Sleep? I'll never be able to, I thought, watching the fog through a hole in the small shack, freezing to death in my wet clothes. No sooner did I finish the thought than I was already snoring.

Voices from the Masks

The next morning we were led to a clearing by a waterfall in a dense forest full of towering trees. While Epigmenio and Philipe got their television equipment ready and Elio tested his tape recorder, a young guerrillero was saying happily, "The voice of the river is going to come through."

Shrouded in clouds, the area was guarded by a column of guerrilleros, all of them had their faces covered by dark woolen ski masks. Their voices and their footsteps sounded muffled.

They arrived, led by Subcomandante Marcos, the person who emerged on January 1st as the EZLN's spokesperson and, until now, its most visible leader — the "talking head" and military strategist. They emerged from the fog: Comandantes Ramona, David, Moisés, Javier, Isaac, and Felipe, dressed in the ceremonial clothes of their respective villages, solemn and unaffected at the same time, with old weapons strung across their chests. They asked us to refrain from taking photographs and describing their clothes, since these could be used to identify their places of origin.

Without being prompted by questions, they took turns weaving a continuous tale about how and why they began their struggle.

Javier began: "We came commissioned as members of the Clandestine Revolutionary Indigenous Committee. Committee because we are organized in collectives. Clandestine because we know there is no place for us in the government, and if the people rise up in armed struggle like this, they know they have no place. That's why we organize this way, secretly. Revolutionary because we are conscious, and there's no other option left but to rise up in arms, to struggle, to see if that way they'll find a solution to our needs. Revolutionary because we want a new society with another way of life.

"The CCRI was founded a long time ago. The fundamental base of our organization is the dire situation our people have been enduring, people who have struggled peacefully with the government, trying to gain the same things as other peoples who have struggled: land titles, housing, and other basic needs. But instead of solving these problems, the government has responded with repression. Our leaders have been beaten, assassinated, exiled, and jailed.

"And so we decided that there was no other option but to organize and rise up this way in armed struggle."

We learned that the plan for the New Year's uprising was put to a vote in all the communities belonging to the Zapatista movement; the majority voted in favor of the uprising.

Isaac recounts, "The people had to be consulted for their opinion; it was they who decided. What would happen if only one group decides to start a war but the people don't support that decision? What if they say no? Well, you can't have the struggle that way.

"It's the people themselves who said, 'Enough, let's begin. We can't take any more because we're already dying of hunger.' So the leaders, the CCRI and the Zapatista Army said, 'If the people say it's time, then it's time. Let's begin.' That's how the struggle began."

Before January 1st the Zapatistas had every intention of waging a peaceful struggle. Isaac points out, "Some people might say we don't have any patience, that we're wrong. We've fought for solutions to our problems in a peaceful way, a legal way. But the government hasn't listened to us. When we took up arms on the first of January, we did it for a good reason. It wasn't to threaten anyone or screw things up. We can recognize who is the enemy of the people and who is their friend. We are respectful of the civilian population."

Regarding political negotiations, which at that time had not yet begun but which were in the process of being established, Moisés says, "We have to consult the people on everything. They've elected us to carry out the revolutionary work. But in other towns, it still seems as though there are not too many people who understand. Why? Because we're advancing in just one part of our state. But we have a lot of hope that we're also carrying the struggle to the state and national levels because the situation we're experiencing is not only specific to our state or a few towns. We know and recognize that our brothers and sisters are suffering the same, in many other towns and many other states."

Regarding land titles, Moisés speaks out again: "In these parts it is a miracle the people are still alive. Families of seven to twelve people have been surviving on a hectare or half a hectare of infertile soil. As campesinos we see and feel an urgent need to have the land in our hands. All the indigenous peoples have been without land for thirty or forty years. But the government has never understood.

"To remedy this situation we would have to implement new laws made by the people themselves. New laws have to be written to divide up the land, perhaps in a way different from what Zapata envisioned — a piece of land for each campesino. We have a better understanding of things now. We know that if you go on giving each person a piece of land, it could just run out. We must find another way of working and organizing. But at any rate, the lands should be turned over to the people. To do this, we'll have to implement new revolutionary laws, written by these people."

Javier addresses democracy and politics: "The governors and politicians know how easy it is to use the indigenous people as a ladder for climbing up to their thrones. Then, once they are in power, safe in their cabinets, they forget about us. Members of the PRI are the only ones who have become this country's governors and presidents. Why have the people supported them? They take advantage of the ignorance caused by illiteracy of the indigenous campesinos. The government specifically knows that the peasants don't know how to analyze the situation correctly, that they'll believe what it tells them. That's why during campaigns, the government hands out gum and candy. The people accept this garbage because of their ignorance, their lack of experience, awareness, and education, their lack of a lot of things.

"That's why this time we're not taking up arms to ask for candy like we did before, or so they'll give us money, or a hat to shade our eyes. What we're asking for is freedom, democracy, and justice."

MP

HUMAN RIGHTS

THE SECRETARIAT FOR HUMAN RIGHTS OF THE Party of the Democratic Revolution (PRD), the principal left opposition party, reports that as of February 1,1994, 263 of their members, activists, and supporters had been assassinated since the beginning of the 1988 electoral campaign.

Torture was frequently used by law-enforcement agents, particularly the state and judicial police, throughout Mexico. Most of the victims were criminal suspects but some — including leaders of indigenous communities and human rights activists — were apparently targeted solely for their peaceful political activities (Amnesty International, 1993).

Over the past four years, Human Rights Watch/Americas Watch and other human rights organizations have documented a consistent pattern of torture and due process abuses in a criminal justice system laced with corruption; electoral fraud and election-related violence; harassment, intimidation, and even violence against independent journalists, human rights monitors, environmentalists, workers, peasants, and indigenous peoples when they seek to exercise their rights to freedom of expression and assembly; and impunity for those who violate fundamental rights (Americas Watch, 1993).

The Mexican Center for Human Rights (CDH) reports that in 1992 and 1993, Chiapas had the highest number of individual rights violations of any state in the nation. CDH claims that "the majority of the aggressions were against Tzeltal and Tzotzil indigenous groups, as well as *mestizo* campesino groups."

INTERVIEW: SUBCOMANDANTE MARCOS

Medea Benjamin

> Antonio dreams that the earth he works belongs to him. He dreams that his sweat is paid with justice and truth. He dreams there is a school to cure ignorance, and medicine to frighten away death. He dreams that reason governs his people and his people govern by reason. In this country everyone dreams. Now the time has come to awaken . . .
>
> *from "Two Winds: A Storm and a Prophecy"*
> *— Subcomandante Marcos*

Can you briefly summarize for the U.S. public what the conflict in Chiapas is all about?

There have been a lot of rumors about the roots of this conflict. Is it about communism? There is no more communism in the world. Fidel Castro? He has too many problems in his own country. The Salvadorans? They're in the midst of a process of reconstruction. The Nicaraguans? The Left is out of power.

The ghost of the American people, the Communist ghost, can no longer be invoked. So now there is another ghost: drug smuggling. Our opponents try to discredit us by saying that we are drug traffickers. But in our army, in our territory, there are no drugs being grown or used. We do not even allow the use of alcohol.

Then what is behind this revolution in Mexico? There is no democracy; you cannot vote for an alternative path. Well, you can vote, but it doesn't mean anything. And this lack of democracy leads to a lot of problems, like political repression, jailings, and killings.

You've spoken about the two Mexicos — the pretty picture of a wealthy Mexico that the PRI tries to promote, and the real Mexico of poverty and misery where Mexico's indigenous people live. Do you think your uprising has helped to reveal the real Mexico?

Exactly. The government has tried to portray Mexico as a First World country. They want to show the World Trade Center, the big malls, the Zona Rosa, the big, modern cities — Acapulco, Cancun, Mexico City, Monterrey, Guadalajara. They want to show the tourists the lovely Mexican culture — the mariachis, the folkloric dancing, the beautiful clothing and crafts of the indigenous people. But behind this picture is the real Mexico, the Mexico of the millions of Indians who live in extreme poverty.

We have helped to peel off the mask to reveal the real Mexico. We've shown that in Chiapas, the Mexican government and a handful of businesses extract all the wealth — the oil, electric energy, tropical trees, cattle, coffee, corn, cacao, bananas. And what do they leave behind? Death and disease — death from curable diseases like respiratory infections, enteritis, parasites, amoebas, malaria, tuberculosis, cholera, and measles. Our uprising was the only way to draw world attention to the poverty and injustices that the indigenous people have been suffering for over 500 years.

What is the most important message you'd like to send to the U.S. government about the conflict?

I know that immigration is a major concern in the United States. Well, this conflict has caused many people to flee and become displaced. They were afraid of the federal army's planes and bombs. In the first weeks of January alone, some twenty thousand people left their homes and became displaced.

Now look at all of Mexico, not just Chiapas. What would happen with immigration to the United States if the conflict was not just in Chiapas? Chiapas has about three million people and Mexico has some ninety million — you can do the multiplication yourself. So the U.S. government should keep in mind that if there is a civil war in Mexico, it doesn't matter how big or thick the wall along the border is. It doesn't matter what material the wall is made out of. If there is a civil war in Mexico, the wall along the U.S. border will come tumbling down.

I would like the U.S. government to know that the Zapatistas are not a threat to the United States. In fact, just the opposite is true. The defeat of the Zapatistas would be a threat. Because the Zapatistas are calling for a democratic Mexico, and if we are defeated, then Mexico won't be moving toward democracy. And it is the lack of democracy that is the real threat, because there is a great deal of discontent in Mexico. Many, many people are fed up and want to see a change in the way our country is run.

What is the best role the United States could play in this process?

The best role would be to stop helping the Mexican government. When the American government comes to the aid of the Mexican government, it positions itself against the Mexican people. When the U.S. government validates fraudulent elections conducted by the Mexican government, it sets itself against the Mexican people.

There is a long history of Mexican mistrust of the U.S. government. In this struggle, where the Mexican people are on one side and the Mexican government is on the other, the United

States must choose sides. Right now, it is on the side of the Mexican government.

The U.S. government has given the Mexican government assistance for the war against drugs. It has trained the police and the army. It has given the government helicopters, communications equipment, and military gear. But the Mexican government is not using this assistance to fight drug traffickers or to track down the leaders of the big drug cartels. It is using this military force to fight against the indigenous people and to repress our struggle for democracy in Mexico.

This is why it is so important for the American people to be aware of what's going on, and to pressure their government to stop supporting the corrupt Mexican government. It's important for the American people to make sure that if another round of violence breaks out, their government will not intervene. Because the United States government doesn't take action without first looking at what the American people think, not since Vietnam. Now, before the U.S. intervenes somewhere, it takes a survey of public opinion. Like in Haiti or the Persian Gulf. First they looked to see what the American people thought before they intervened.

What were the influences that moved you to do what you're doing? Were you influenced by the works of Marx and Lenin?

(He laughs) My main influences were Villa, Zapata, Morelos, Hidalgo, Guerrero. My parents taught me a lot about Mexican history; I grew up with these heroes. My parents also taught me that whatever path I chose in life, I should always choose the path of truth, no matter how hard it might be. I was taught that human beings all had rights, that there was a lot of injustice in the world, and that the duty of human beings was to fight against injustice.

Are there lessons you learned from the Cuban revolution?

Well, I don't know if you can call them lessons, because we didn't take Cuba as our frame of reference. But we learned that you can't impose a form of politics on the people because sooner or later you'll end up doing the same thing that you criticized. You criticize a totalitarian system and then offer another totalitarian system. You can't impose a political system by force.

There's a big difference between the guerrilla movements of the fifties, sixties, and seventies, and those of today. Before, they said, "Let's get rid of this system of government and put in this other kind of system." We say, "No, the political system can't be the product of a war." The war should only be to open up space in the political arena so that the people can really have a choice. It doesn't matter who wins, it doesn't matter if it's the extreme Right or the extreme Left, as long as they earn the confidence of the people.

Would you really be happy to make these incredible sacrifices so that an ultraright party could come to power?

We want to create the political space, and we want the people to have the education and the political maturity to make good choices.

Speaking of education, what is the average amount of schooling in this area?

In the Zapatista Army, about 75 percent of our soldiers are illiterate, both in Spanish and in their own language. Here there are no schools to go to. And if there is a school, the teacher almost never shows up because it's too far. If you are a teacher in one of these remote villages, you must walk along muddy paths for days just to get to the school. And you must teach children who are falling asleep in class because they are so weak and hungry. Or the children don't show up because they have to go and cut wood or do other chores.

Is there still the feeling here that the more children you have, the more people there are to help with the family chores and work the land?

Yes, many people have a very contradictory logic. They want the children because they help with the harvest, but then those children grow up, get married, and want their own land, but there is no more land to give them. So in the long run it doesn't make sense to have many children. But there is this contradiction. It makes sense from one point of view and doesn't make sense from another.

A campesino who was a Zapatista sympathizer told me that the government wants to get rid of the Indians, and so the Indians should have as many children as possible, so they can help get rid of the government.

(He laughs) Yes, people make jokes about that. And it's true that there are many women who start to have children very early, at the age of thirteen or fourteen, but that is something we discourage.

What's the average number of children per family here?

About eight to ten, and maybe three or four of them will die.

So do you talk about this with the villagers?

Yes, we recommend that young girls don't have children. Many of the women here think it's good to only have a few children. They want contraceptives but they don't have access to them. They ask us for help, because they know that the women who are Zapatista fighters use contraceptives. We give them out when we have them, but we don't have enough to give to everyone who wants them.

The Zapatista women have drafted a law on women's rights. Can you talk about the issues this document deals with?

Here in this region the women cannot choose their mates. They are bought with a dowry. If I want to marry you, I must pay a goat or a pig. And our women have said, no more — that they now have the right to choose their partner and cannot be forced into marriage. This is an enormous change.

Another new law is that women now have the right to participate in the affairs of the community and to hold positions of authority if they are democratically elected. The men protested this, but they had to give in. Because the women bargained, saying they would only support the issues that the men wanted if the men approved these changes.

Then there's the issue of birth control. This law says that women can control the number of children they have, and the men can't say no. It also says that women cannot be beaten or physically mistreated, and that rape will be severely punished. These are all very revolutionary changes for the women here.

You often talk about the need for a better distribution of land in Chiapas as critical for improving the lives of the indigenous people. But, given the growing population, is there really enough land to go around?

That's why the principal demand we have is not for more land, but to get assistance to increase the productivity of the land we have. The land we have is very depleted, so why should we get more if we're going to have the same problems? It's not a question of just getting a piece of land, but of getting technical assistance for the land we already have.

Isn't one of your demands that you want to get better land?

In some situations, yes. Some of the land is pure rock, and there's nothing you can do with it. It's very bad land, way up in the mountains. But some of the land is like it is right here, what they call *planadas*, which are flatter, or the banks of the rivers, which is where the cattle ranches are. But those are not very fertile anymore either, because they've been used for grazing for too long. But if we had tractors, fertilizers, good seeds, technical assistance, this land would produce eight to sixteen times what it produces now. Right now, we get half a ton of corn per hectare when we should be getting an average of seven or eight tons.

What about those who don't have land?

We need to have collective farms. We think the big farms should be given over to production collectives that would use some of their produce for their own sustenance and sell the rest. So we're not talking about distributing land into little parcels, but turning the big farms into production collectives and increasing productivity by using better farming techniques.

Here there is no advanced technology at all. People farm with a stick. They don't even have oxen. For example, the land of one ranch might be the equivalent of the land of an *ejido*, but it produces more. Why? Because the ranch owner has tools, a tractor, better education, so the land produces more.

I've heard you say things that seem contradictory about the origins of the EZLN as a fighting force. Sometimes you say that you started organizing for the armed struggle; other times you say that you started organizing for self-defense, for protection against the cattle ranchers' armed security forces, and that you only took the offensive due to changing circumstances — like electoral fraud and the changes in Article 27 of the Constitution.

When we first came here, we talked about the issue of armed struggle. And the indigenous people said, "Yes, we have to take up arms to defend ourselves." So we began to train for self-defense, not for how to attack. That's how the Zapatista National

Liberation Army was born, as a self-defense force. And that's how we grew. Our objective in training in the mountains has been to protect the villagers.

But in 1992, the situation changed. That year there was a lot of organizing in the indigenous communities about to commemorate the five hundred years of resistance since the landing of Christopher Columbus in the Americas. That's when the indigenous people of this region said, "We've already been struggling for five hundred years. It's time to say 'enough.'" They voted in their communities, and the decision was made to go to war.

They told me to start the war, because I was the one in charge of military planning. I said that we couldn't, that we weren't ready. I said that we needed time, because all of our training was for defense, while they now wanted to attack the cities. So I asked them for more time to organize. In January of 1993, they said they would give me one year to make the arrangements. "If you don't do it in a year, we'll do it without you," they said. They told me that the latest date was December 31, 1993. It had to be sometime between January and December.

So in 1993 we had to readjust our entire military system to organize for the offensive. That's when we prepared the second string of leaders, because according to our organizational concept, the leaders must lead the troops in combat, in order to have moral authority. But we thought that the first string of leaders would be killed in the first days of combat. We thought that all of us leading the troops would die — me, the other officers, and the members of the committees. So we had to prepare the second string of military leaders and committee members as replacements, and this second string had to be hidden away.

So then what happened? We went out, we fought, and they didn't kill us. That's the great surprise, that they didn't kill us in that first week of January (he laughs).

So you were prepared for a suicide mission?

No, I wouldn't call it that. You commit suicide when you think life isn't worth living. You say, "I'm tired of living, I'm depressed," and you shoot yourself in the head. That's not our case. We want to keep on living, but we knew that we had to do something so that others might live. This is about taking risks so that others can live. Maybe we would die in the effort, we knew that there was a good possibility of that. But we were not on a suicide mission. We were prepared to die, but we didn't want to die.

And we didn't think we would all die. Only the leaders, and then others would take our place.

Many people in the United States say you chose January 1st to attack because that was the day that the North American Free Trade Agreement went into effect. Was this planned, or just a coincidence?

Yes, some Americans sent me a letter asking why we waited, saying that we should have attacked before, when the agreement was still under discussion.

Yes, if NAFTA were your objective, it would have been more logical to make the offensive when the agreement was still being discussed in the U.S. Congress.

Yes, but we were not prepared. We were going to make the offensive on October 12, but the army discovered our arms cache up in the mountains, a five- or six-hour walk from here. So we had to pull back and postpone our plans until December.

We came up with three different possible dates. We knew that the best time to attack would be a holiday, when there are festivities and lots of people around, and when the soldiers would be relaxing. October 12, the day of the Virgin of Guadalupe, was a possibility because there are a lot of pilgrimages that day. So we thought that we could get the troops into town as if they were civilians going to see the Virgin of Guadalupe, while they were really going in to attack the cities. But we weren't ready, and in fact, the compañeros did go to see the Virgin of Guadelupe (laughter).

Then the next possible date was the night of December 24, for Christmas. But the committee decided that since it was a religious date, an attack might be interpreted as being antireligious. I only had a few days left. So I chose December 28, because the 28th is Día de los Inocentes [Fools' Day] and people play a lot of practical jokes on that day. I thought, "That's good. When the soldiers call and say they're being attacked, the general's going to think they're playing a trick on him, and he'll hang up" (laughing). But then I thought that when the journalists reported the attack, the same thing would happen, no one would believe them. So we decided to postpone the date again, until the 31st.

Even if the attack wasn't timed for the beginning of NAFTA, was NAFTA still an important factor in your decision to rise up?

Yes, as I have said, NAFTA is a death sentence for the indigenous people. NAFTA sets up competition among farmers, but how can our campesinos — who are mostly illiterate — compete with U.S. and Canadian farmers? And look at this rocky land we have here. How can we compete with the land in California, or in Canada? So the people of Chiapas, as well as the people of Oaxaca, Veracruz, Quintana Roo, Guerrero, and Sonora were the sacrificial lambs of NAFTA.

Did the campesinos here fight against NAFTA from the time it was proposed?

No, because the campesinos here were busy fighting against the reforms in Article 27. So there were two attacks, one to the head, another to the stomach, and the campesinos were busy worrying about their stomachs. Also, we thought that the problems in passing NAFTA were going to come more from the American people than from the Mexican people. We really didn't think that NAFTA was going to pass in the United States.

The reforms of Article 27 were meant to modernize the Mexican countryside. And yes, its final objective was to prepare for the NAFTA agreement. But we saw NAFTA as very uncertain because of the campaign against it in the United States. So no one paid a lot of attention to it — in the last instance it was going to be determined by what happened in the United States. Even if the Mexican government said yes, it still had to be ratified in the United States And this was not certain until the very end. People kept saying, "Maybe it won't pass, maybe it won't pass."

When you started in January, did you ever think this movement would become so great and would capture all of Mexico?

What would you have thought if I had said to you on December 31, "Tomorrow morning we're going to launch an attack on eight municipalities. We're going to start a war with the objective of overthrowing the Mexican government and installing a transition government that would hold free and fair elections. If I said that we're going to have ten thousand people in arms, and have many more in reserve, what would you say to me?

You're crazy.

Exactly. You'd say that armed struggle doesn't work anymore, that we'd never be able to win, etc. It's not a logical thing to do. But there are things you can't understand until they happen (he laughs).

People say that the key to the Zapatistas' success so far is that you, Marcos, have been such an effective bridge between the indigenous and nonindigenous worlds. You have also become one of Latin

America's most brilliant — and prolific — writers. How in the world, in the midst of running a war . . . ?

I think it's the kind of life I'm leading now that makes me write (he draws a line in the dirt). On one side is life and on the other is death. And since January 1st, I'm right on the border. I can easily pass to the other side any day now. So I can't have any ambitions to write a great novel or to have some great career. The only thing I'm sure of is this moment. So while I never wrote anything before, now I write as if every day were the last.

It's become a compulsion to put out everything that I have inside. I have so much built up inside me from these ten years that I've lived in this part of the country. With this immediate sense of death, I feel as if I were unstopped, like a soda that's been shaken up for a long time and then the cap is taken off. Being on the edge between life and death causes this kind of explosion in me.

Given your role of spokesperson and how incisive you are, aren't you worried that the EZLN has become too closely associated with one person? Whether or not you like it, there is now a Marcos personality cult that can be detrimental to the long-term health of the movement.

This is a complicated issue. First of all, what do I gain from this personality cult? Nothing. Women don't come here for me — just journalists like you (laughing). There are no sexual benefits in this for me, I don't sell books on myself, I don't make any money off this image. In the end, I don't gain anything personally. It is the movement that benefits, because this way more people pay attention to the issue.

And secondly, no one knows who Marcos is anyway. This Marcos does not even have a face. Even the people I've been living with here for years don't know my background. They only know my face and they know that I am called Marcos. Nothing more. If you ask them, "Where is Marcos from?" they'll say, "I don't know. From the mountains."

So if they kill me, someone else can put on the mask and say they're Marcos. This way there will always be a Marcos.

Why did you take the name Marcos?

It was the name of a friend of mine who was killed. He was killed at a military checkpoint in the road.

So it doesn't mean "Movimiento Armado Revolucionario Comandante Obispo Samuel" *[Comandante Bishop Samuel's Armed Revolutionary Movement]?*

(He laughs) Nor Margaritas, Altamirano, Rancho Nuevo, Comitán, Ocosingo, San Cristóbal [local towns in Chiapas which were occupied during the Zapatista uprising].

When will you take off your mask?

If I take my mask off, there will be even more of a personality cult because I'm so good-looking (laughter).

No, really, I've said that I will take off my ski mask when Mexican society takes off its own mask, the one it uses to cover up the real Mexico. Then Mexicans would see that the self-image they have been sold is false, and that the reality of Mexico is much more terrible than they'd ever imagined. And once they have seen the real Mexico — as we have seen it — they will be more determined to change it.

INTERVIEW:
BISHOP SAMUEL RUIZ GARCÍA
Paulina Hermosillo

IN SOUTHEASTERN MEXICO, DAY AFTER DAY, PEOPLE live in thinly disguised slavery. Landed cattlemen, ranch owners, and *ladinos* are the main oppressors of more than 885,000 indigenous peasants, among them Tzeltales, Tzotziles, Ch'oles, Tojolabales, Zoques, Mames, Zapotecos, and Lacandones.

"When this kind of oppression is in place for years, centuries, when the rights of indigenous peasants and campesinos are not recognized and there's even some doubt as to whether or not they have a soul . . . what alternative was left to them? There was no other way out," points out the bishop of the Diocese of San Cristóbal de Las Casas, Samuel Ruiz García, when accounting for the causes that brought about the conflict. "In this diocese, we serve the poor, who make up 80 percent of the population.

We have to be on the side of those who are suffering the most. We found ourselves needing to build an authentic church. The church is not a list of dogmatic truths that have to be followed, nor a set of moral rules, although there is an ethic to follow in what is a history of salvation.

"They didn't have a history, because those who are dominated do not have a history, it's the history of the dominator. How could we lay a foundation for a church where there wasn't even a historical consciousness, where there was no subject? That was the leap from a cultish church to one of authentic social commitment." Quoting from his pastoral letter, Samuel Ruiz declares, "The indigenous world, greater in their percentual majority and in their marginalization, demanded of us — if we wanted to be loyal to the Gospel — an urgent response.

"As an indigenous man told me years ago, if the church does not make itself Tzeltal with the Tzeltales, Ch'ol with the Ch'oles, Tojolabal with the Tojolabales, I don't understand how it can call itself the Catholic church. It would be, in effect, a foreign church, belonging to a dominant social class. . . . It should be fully understood that the kingdom of God is not constructed in eternity, although it ends there, but that it's built here, starting with the poor, that is what Jesus preached.

"If it's theology, it can't be 'theology of slavery.' Christ came to liberate humanity. As a pastor, I care little for theology, what's important to me is liberation. You ask what's behind all this? Well, it's slavery wanting to be perpetuated. And all Christian liberation leads to liberation from slavery."

AM

RELIGION AND EXPULSIONS

REPRESENTATIVES OF THE PROGRESSIVE CATHOLIC church, mainly the Bishop of San Cristóbal de las Casas, Samuel Ruiz García, and his group of priests and catechists, have been repeatedly accused of stirring up unrest among the Indian population as a result of their work in defense of the Indians' rights, based on the principles of liberation theology. With over thirty years in the area, Samuel Ruiz has gained the affection and admiration of hundreds of Indians, but also the enmity and antagonism of cattle ranchers, local rulers, and government officials who regard him as an agitator of Indians. The bishop acknowledges that he has worked to make the Indians aware of the need to defend their rights and fight to improve their living conditions through their own organizations, as well as to recover their dignity and appreciation of their own customs and cultures, although he states that taking up arms is not the best way to fight. In his pastoral letter of August 6, 1993 (a copy of which was personally delivered to Pope John Paul II during his last visit to Mexico in September 1993), Samuel Ruiz denounced the state of dependency, marginalization, and oppression in which the Indians are held (*Proceso*, January 24, 1994).

The bishop's position led to attempts by the papal representative in Mexico, Girolamo Prigione, to obtain his removal. The Indians, with the support of grassroots organizations both in Mexico and abroad, demanded he should stay. This helped to polarize social groups in the state.

At the same time, the heightened presence of other religious groups has served as a pretext for a complex problem in the state:

expulsions. The best example of this is the Chamula community, located a few miles from San Cristóbal, where, under the pretext that the "new religions" contradict Catholic customs, respecting neither patriotic symbols nor civil authority, thousands of inhabitants have been expelled from their lands and prevented from returning. These expulsions have prompted all kinds of violence, theft, pillage, rape, imprisonment, and even the burning of houses and belongings.

"For more than twenty years, the *expulsados* [people who have been expelled] have complained to governors and courts about these outrages, whose main aim is to eliminate resistance to the *caciques*, yet so far they have never obtained a satisfactory response. . . . The *caciques* in San Juan Chamula are highly aware politically and know that during electoral periods they can do as they please. . . . In 1987 and 1988, election years at the state and national levels, one expulsion followed another. . . . In the courts, lawsuits against the expellers had no effect, because the *caciques* in Chamula threatened not to vote for the PRI [in 1988], again the *caciques* 'won the war'. . . . It is estimated that twenty thousand Indians have been expelled and scattered throughout a dozen municipalities in the state. . . . The local deputy from San Cristóbal, Francisco Zepeda, asked the *expulsados* to 'forgive their brothers who expelled them, because they are all God's children,' offering them land on a small farm outside San Juan Chamula as a solution to the conflict" (Gaspar Morquecho in *La Jornada*, February 7, 10, 12, and 13, 1994).

CHAMULA CARNAVAL, 1994
Xunka Utz'utz'ni'

THE FESTIVAL OF CARNAVAL DIDN'T GO WELL THIS
year. It was sad because the Federal Army had forbidden the use
of fireworks, and they were going around saying that the
Zapatistas would invade during the festival — on the 12th, 13th,
or 14th of February. Everyone in all the *parajes* — Los Pasiones,
Los Mayordomos, Los Alféreses — was saying the same thing,
that the Zapatistas were coming, along with the *expulsados* from
La Hormiga and Colonia Paraíso. They were coming to kill us all
at the festival in Chamula. They were going to bomb us on the
Sunday of Carnaval. We wouldn't survive; it would be the end of
our story.

So the people from Los Pasiones lit candles in the church and
on every mountain, to block the way for the Zapatistas and to

make the festival go well. They lit candles and prayed on the mountain of Milpoleta, Chaklajún, where the old ones tell us there are many guns inside the mountain. They say that Obregón y Pineda's soldiers went in there a long time ago, who knows how many years ago. The mountain swallowed them up and they remained inside, along with their weapons. Everyone knows that mountain is full of soldiers. Their flesh, their bodies have already been finished off by worms or vultures, who knows, but their spirits are still there in that cave. They're still there today, with their guns. But the spirits don't kill anymore. When it thunders, it's Obregón y Pineda's guns that are shooting. The spirits of the soldiers don't do anything anymore; they don't know how to kill now.

Since January, when the news came that there were guerrilleros in San Cristóbal, all the Chamulas had been saying they weren't afraid. That's a lie, of course they were. To hide it, everyone said that the one who should really be afraid for his sins, the only one responsible for all of the violent transgressions in Chamula was the mayor. Well, of course, in their hearts everyone knew that they had also participated in the expulsions of the Evangelicals, and everyone feared a settling of accounts. They were also afraid that the Zapatistas wouldn't waste time talking; since they had good weapons, a lot of Chamulas were going to die.

What to do? The Chamulas don't have decent weapons, just 22-caliber rifles, pistols, and one or two old shotguns. Forget it, instead of fighting, they should hide themselves under their beds. The mayor was so scared, thinking of what his expelled countrymen would do to him if they caught him, that he walked around in a daze for about a week. He knew better than anyone what he had done. But not just him. All of the authorities feared the arrival of the Zapatistas. To tell the truth, the whole town was afraid.

Then, since there was no other form of defense, the mayor went to light candles and incense in the mountains, to ask for the protection of God and the saints. The Chamula sorcerers are powerful, and authorities and important people from Zinacantán, Amatenango, San Miguel Mitontic, and Huixtán came to participate as well. They all came to pray in Chamula, on the mountain of Chaklajún. From there, they went to the church and on to the sacred hills of Zinacantán. They thought that together, they would have the power to stop the EZLN, to keep them from entering any of their communities.

This is more or less what they prayed on Chaklajún:

Hear us, Sacred Lightning,
Hear us, Sacred Mountain,
Hear us, Sacred Thunder,
Hear us, Sacred Cave,
We come to awaken your conscience
We come to awaken your heart.
We want to borrow your feet
We want to borrow your hands
To shoot your rifle
To fire your cannon
To close off our road
To those, your sons,
To close off our road
To those, your daughters,
Though they come in the night
Though they come in the day
Though they come at sundown
Though they come at daybreak,
Though they come at midnight,
Señor.
Bring us a rifle
Bring us a machete

Bring us a pistol, Señor.
Do you not see that we are here,
Sacred Lightning?
Do you not see that we are here,
Sacred Thunder?
Give us your rifle,
Give us your cannon,
Oh exalted San Juan
Exalted protector.
Sacred guardian of the earth
Sacred guardian of heaven.
We have traveled over
Huitepec Mountain,
We have traveled by
Sakch'enal,
Holy Father
We have passed by San Cristóbal Mountain
Holy Mother
Don't let them onto your land,
Great Protector.
Let their rifles freeze
Let their cannons freeze,
Señor.
Accept this little branch of flowers
Accept this offering of leaves, Señor
Accept this offering of smoke,
Sacred Lightning,
Sacred Mountain,
Sacred Cave,
Holy Father of Chaklajún
Holy Mother of Chaklajún.

That's how we asked the angel, the lightning — well, that which is the owner of the cave — for the guns to thunder inside the mountain, to block the road so the Zapatistas wouldn't enter Chamula during Carnaval. The Evangelical Chamulas, the *expulsados* as we call them, also were afraid of the Zapatistas. Since they live in colonies on the outskirts of San Cristóbal, they had seen them up close and had been frightened. They were also afraid of the weapons of the Federal Army, and they prayed, too:

Nuestro Señor Jesus Christ,
God who is in heaven,
Here they come, bearing arms,
Here they come, carrying machetes, Señor.
Look at us,
See us,
On your path,
On our long walk, Señor.
Don't let them come to hit us,
Don't let them come to torture us
In our houses,
In our homes.
Alleluia, Alleluia, Alleluia.

Translation from Tzotzil to Spanish by Jan Rus.

EK

WHO ARE THEY, WHAT DO THEY WANT?

John Ross

AFTER THE CIVIC FIREWORKS AND THE SANCTIMO-
nious explosion of church bells, the tourists toddled off to warm
beds and bottles and their own private parties. The empty stone
streets of the old colonial city glistened with icy mountain mist
as 1994 rolled in over the Chiapas highlands.

The velvet black midnight was suddenly stippled with silent,
darting shapes. At precisely 00:30 of the New Year, the slap-slap
of rubber boots against slick pavement echoed through the
Indian barrios on the edge of town. Across the Puente Blanco
and down the Diagonal Centenario, dark shadows jogged in military cadence. With their features concealed behind ski masks
and red bandanas, leaving their breath hanging in the cold, still
air like the living vapors of Mayan ghosts, the Zapatistas

advanced on the strategic center of San Cristóbal de las Casas. In this tourist hideaway crowning the Mayan highlands of Chiapas, the rebels declared war upon the government of Mexico in the name of the martyred revolutionary hero, Emiliano Zapata, and the first post–Cold War uprising of the poor of Latin America had begun.

Who were these shadows from a past that many of the more modern Mexicans had thought was long since dead?

~

The Mexican army is viscerally angry, *encabronado* [made to feel like an enraged cuckold]. On the fifth day of the rebellion, MONITOR Radio correspondent Sandina Robbins climbs up to San Antonio de los Baños, high on the cold, pine-treed slopes south of San Cristóbal. The village seems abandoned, chickens and dogs sniffing and scratching in the empty dirt streets. Suddenly, the gut-tightening silence is shattered by a pair of jet fighters streaking in low from the west, strafing the high pine forest just outside the hamlet. There is a long, piercing whistle and an angry boom, and the ground shakes perilously under Sandina's shoes as the rockets plow into the hillside. The reporter dives for cover in the doorway of a nearby hovel. Inside, four Tzotzil women are huddled in the corner, gasping for air but insisting they are not afraid. One pulls out her plastic voter registration card, the new kind that has the bearer's picture imprinted on it, and shakes it at the heavens. "*Somos del PRI!*" [We're with the PRI !] she screams. "*Somos del PRI! Del PRI! Del PRI!*" echo her terrified compañeras.

~

On the first morning that the road slicing towards Ocosingo is open, we ease past the military roadblock to inspect the carnage that the Mexican army has inflicted in the week that the war zone has been sealed off to public witness. Outside of the

Chiapas State Social Rehabilitation Center Number 5, from which the Zapatistas freed nearly two hundred indigenous prisoners, Mai Ying videographs a crumpled bus in which fourteen unarmed young rebels were machine-gunned on the third morning of the war. The army left their riddled bodies to rot on the side of the road for days, my colleagues say, as a warning to others who might be inclined to rise up in arms against the Mexican state. Now the bodies are gone and we prowl the empty, splintered interior of the bus that is embroidered everywhere with dried pools of blood and shards of glass.

Juan Carlos offers to narrate how the boys were killed. "Wait! I don't speak Spanish," Mai Ying protests. I grumpily offer to translate. The soldiers are just over the hill. None of us has good identification. Juan Carlos begins again, telling how the young men died. How the U.S.-made helicopter gunship roared down the valley, spraying the rebels with machine-gun tracers. "It all happened very quickly." He does not know their names.

We encounter five Indian women, out hunting down a strayed cow. They walk single file on the shoulder of the highway. Two of them are leading black dogs on strands of bright green ribbon. They speak excitedly in click-tongued Tzotzil. Then, in broken Spanish, the women tell us that they have just found a corpse and take us into the forest to view the remains.

The dead man has been eaten by dogs and turkey vultures and only his glistening ribcage and the skeletal structure of his skull is still intact. Like all the half-eaten dead in this land where on every Day of the Dead, the *muertitos* get up and dance, he seems to be grinning.

Who was he? What was his name? Someone says the dead man must have been here since the battle of Rancho Nuevo. He is certainly a Zapatista — the white bones of his legs are still planted in rubber boots, the emblematic footwear of this ragtag army of liberation.

We turn back to the vacant highway, leaving the dead Zapatista behind in the forest to mulch with the generations of bones that dwell beneath this wedge of earth. Rancho Nuevo, the site of the 31st Military Zone of the Mexican army, was built upon a Tzotzil graveyard.

~

We arrive in Ocosingo on the thirteenth day of the uprising. A ceasefire has been declared, but the military is uneasy. Long lines of small, colorfully dressed Tzeltal women wait patiently as the soldiers hand out plastic bags containing sardine tins, rice, sugar, and cooking oil. There are not enough bags for the hundreds of women who have gathered in the park, and the soldiers nervously shout at them not to get too close. Behind the troops, the destroyed City Hall still smolders fitfully.

The women have been standing in line since early morning and the distribution moves at an excruciatingly slow pace. Each recipient must show her voter registration card to receive the food and each is questioned about the whereabouts of their husbands and their fathers, their sons and their brothers. The men, it is murmured, are either dead and buried in hastily dug common graves, or else they have fled into the jungle with the Zapatistas.

~

Who are the Zapatistas? They strip off their rubber boots and red *paliacates* and slip back onto the *ejidos* in the canyons and the jungle as if they had never been gone. All over the state of Chiapas, the campesinos have either taken heart from the rebels or else they are themselves the ones *sin rostros* [without faces] who have put on a mask and invaded the *fincas* [plantations], planting their banner in the middle of cornfields and rich pasturelands, where one prize bull grazes on dozens of green acres.

The small, white, landowning elite that preserves Chiapas as its own private estate in which the Indians still belong to the *fincas*, accuse the bishop of San Cristóbal of fomenting insurrection. The bishop, a small, chunky man who looks a little like Yoda, says Mass and writes pastoral letters decrying the poverty of the Indian faithful. The pope does not like him.

As the *Guardias Blancas* [White Guards: private security forces] of the ranchers' associations prepare to expel the invaders from private property, other struggles are recalled. The names of Andulio Galvaz and Sebastian Nuñez, Joel Padrón and Arturo Albores are still written on the whitewashed adobe walls of Comitán and Simojovel. This has been a long war, the *sin rostros* remind us, this war didn't just begin on New Year's Eve.

～

Who are the Zapatistas? They speak from "the mountains of the southeast of Mexico" and from "somewhere in the Lacandón jungle." They say the Clandestine Revolutionary Indigenous Committee — the all-Indian general command of the EZLN — speaks through Subcomandante Marcos, but Marcos often seems to speak for himself. The man in the ski mask, the only *ladino* in the Zapatista hierarchy, is a sophisticated, city-bred poet with a flair for Grand Guignol. With red-tipped bandoleras crisscrossed over his black *chuj*, Marcos sits in the gilded San Cristóbal cathedral, briskly smoking his pipe through the mouth-slot of his ski mask, as peace talks between the government and the heavily armed rebels begin.

Three hundred "news gatherers" have been accredited to attend the talks. When Marcos arrives from the jungle, they are there to greet him. Like a movie starlet on Oscar night, the subcomandante hikes up his pants to show some leg when he enters the Cathedral of Peace and the cameras click in thunderous unison.

~

Months later, in the backwaters of the Lacandón, Marcos is still in demand. He gives an interview to *Vanity Fair* and tells tall tales of sexual exploits to the *San Francisco Chronicle.* He rejects the government's peace offer and calls for a Democratic National Convention. He communicates with famous authors and tells the urbane Carlos Monsiváis that his job "is to make war and write letters."

In his spare time, Marcos writes fables for children in far-away cities. In one story, he converses with a beetle who has been stealing his tobacco. The beetle is concerned that his brothers and sisters are being stepped upon by big men in boots. "When is this war going to be over?" he asks the subcomandante. Not soon, he is told.

~

Who are the Zapatistas? They seem suddenly to be everywhere in the land. In all of the Indian sierras, masked men and women are sighted, but never quite materialize. Indigenous leaders voice solidarity with the rebels and threaten to join up if their own demands are not met. Farmers in central Mexico block the highways with their tractors and close down banks in solidarity. In January, over one hundred thousand Zapatista supporters fill the great Zócalo of Mexico City, and on one day in February there are 102 marches in the capital, alone. Truckers park sixty huge rigs in the Zócalo, the enormous plaza that has been at the heart of Mexican reality since it was called Tenochtitlán, when the Aztec-Mexicas ruled the empire. They pump on air horns, augmenting the aura of general insurrection.

At the Metropolitan Book Fair that same weekend, young people who are pissed off because a token admission is being charged for the first time in fourteen years, push their way into the main salon, chanting, "Marcos! Marcos!" And just down the street, at the slowly deconstructing Palacio de Bellas Artes, where Verdi's "Nabuco" — a potent political opera — is being performed, an excited aficionado rises in the second balcony and hollers at the top of his lungs, "*Que Viven los Zapatistas!*"

"*Que Viven!*" the upscale, elegantly-coiffed audience on the floor of Bellas Artes responds.

~

Who are these new Zapatistas? That's what Emetario Pantaleón, ninety-seven, wants to know. "What do these muchachos want?" Don Emetario asks. We are sitting in the doorway of his house, just up the street from the home of Emiliano Zapata, now a glass-and-concrete-enclosed adobe shell, a government museum and the pride of Anenecuilco, in the state of Morelos, the land for which Zapata fought and fought. Emetario Pantaleón stood at his general's side — or at least he carried water and ammunition at the battle of Iguala, 1913. He is one of the oldest members of the *ejido*, but not the oldest, a *veterano* who still rides ramrod-stiff up to his land each morning, and does not return until the sun is setting.

In the warm Anenecuilco evening, Emetario Pantaleón will talk to you a long time about the old Zapatistas, will tell you how fearless and noble they were, and point reverentially to their fading portraits on his wall. But he doesn't know about these new Zapatistas. "The Army has a lot of weapons, a lot of ammunition — these boys are going to get all the poor people killed . . ." The new Zapatistas aren't serious, thinks Emetario Pantaleón. "I've seen the dead stacked up all the way from here to Osumba, under the volcano," he remembers sadly. "These muchachos are just boys. They don't think they are ever going to die."

~

Months after their New Year's Day fiesta sent shivers galloping down the spine of Mexico's rulers, the Zapatistas are penned between the mountains and the jungle, their butts up against the Guatemalan border, surrounded on three sides by a Mexican army that has, thus far, resisted its more homicidal impulses to annihilate them. Militarily, the Zapatistas are outflanked and politically, their influence has been upstaged by a spectacular violence so close to the surface of Mexico's highly stratified society, incarnated in the shadowy assassination of President Carlos Salinas's anointed heir, far away at the other end of the republic, in Tijuana. Marcos, the genial myth in the eye of this overdue whirlwind, sends gloomy communiqués to the international press saying, "Our cycle is coming to a close . . ." But the Zapatistas have been outgunned from the first moment of their revolution and still they survive in the hearts and minds of their compatriots.

Back in January, I sat watching kids skitter around a shabby, dimly lit plaza in San Cristóbal, ducking behind park benches and shooting at each other with homemade wooden versions of the automatic weapons so much in evidence in the highlands these days. "Who are the Zapatistas and who are the soldiers of the Mexican Army?" I ask them. "I am the Zapatista," laughs a slender ten-year-old in ragged clothing, "and they are the *soldados*," — he jerked his chin at an older boy and a girl younger than himself, perhaps his sister.

"And who will win?"

"They have two guns and I only have this one," the boy said gravely, brandishing his carefully crafted weapon, "but there is no doubt. I must win."

THE SUBCOMANDANTE OF PERFORMANCE

Guillermo Gómez Peña

I

MEXICO CITY WAS HUNG OVER. EARLY IN THE morning of January 1, 1994, its inhabitants were recuperating from the epic New Year's celebrations. Turning on my television, I was suddenly confronted with images of guerrilleros that resembled the Sandinista upheaval of the late seventies and the Salvadoran civil war. First, I thought it was a documentary about Central America. Then, an excited reporter announced that "an armed group calling itself the Zapatista National Liberation Army has taken over the city of San Cristóbal de las Casas, and several small villages in the jungle of Chiapas." My heart began to pound rapidly. I phoned my friends. They thought I was kidding.

What made the Zapatista insurrection different from any other recent Latin American guerrilla movement was its self-conscious and sophisticated use of the media. From the onset, the EZLN was fully aware of the symbolic power of their military actions. They chose to strategically begin the war precisely on the day that NAFTA went into effect. And since the second day of the conflict, they placed as much importance on staging press conferences and theatrical photos as on their military strategy. The war was carried on as if it were performance. Most of the Zapatistas, indigenous men, women, and children, wore *pasamontañas* [black ski masks]. Some utilized wooden rifles as mere props. One of the leaders, Subcomandante Marcos, turned out to be a consummate *performancero*. He was undoubtedly the latest popular hero in a noble tradition of activists which includes Superbarrio, Fray Tormenta (the wrestler priest), and Super-Ecologista, all self-proclaimed "social wrestlers" who have utilized performance and media strategies to enter in the political "wrestling arena" of contemporary Mexico.

II

Since his first appearances in the media, Marcos, otherwise known as "*el Sup*," appealed to the most diverse and unlikely sectors of Mexican society. In the confusing era of "the end of ideology," his utopian political visions — presented in simple, nonideological, and poetic language — went straight to the jaded hearts and minds of students, activists, intellectuals, artists, nihilistic teens, and even apolitical middle-class professionals. In an era of ferocious neonationalisms, he made sure to avoid nationalist jargon and dogmas. His combination of political clarity, bravado, and humility appealed to progressive politicians and activists throughout the world. His eclectic discourse, spiced with humor and a surprising array of references to pop culture, contemporary writers, and world news revealed a sophisticated internationalism. Despite all this, he remained humble. (He defines himself as a mere "sub," a kind of secretary of public relations, an interpreter to the outside world.) His serious but nonchalant demeanor, adorned with a pipe and a Zapata-style bandolera with bullets that don't match the model of his weapon, made him extremely photogenic. His persona was a carefully crafted collage of twentieth-century revolutionary symbols, costumes, and props borrowed from Zapata, Sandino, Che, and Arafat as well as from celluloid heroes such as Zorro and Mexico's movie wrestler, "El Santo." Because of all this, the *New York Times* christened him "the first postmodern guerrilla leader," and newspapers and magazines throughout the world made it a priority to obtain an interview with him. The cult of Marcos was born.

El Sup planned his relationship with the media very carefully. The international press was a priority, of course. *Der Spiegel, Cambio 16, Le Figaro,* the *New York Times,* the *San Francisco Chronicle, NACLA,* and *Vanity Fair* were immediately welcomed into the jungle. In regards to the Mexican press, he was a bit more cautious. He favored the two independent dailies, *La Jornada* and *El Financiero,* and developed a direct line of communication with them. He also put a lot of emphasis on radio, since for most of the indigenous communities of Chiapas and throughout rural Mexico it is the main source of information. The pro-government media conglomerate, Televisa, was banned from the press conferences and peace talks. And this, of course, was an act of defiance that Televisa couldn't accept. Their reporters did everything they could to get close to him. They tried to sneak in as members of other TV networks. And when they couldn't, they bought footage from European television. The results of this publicity campaign were extraordinary. In a month, Marcos became a household name around the world.

An industry of Zapatista and Marcos-inspired souveneirs flourished overnight. T-shirts, ski-mask condoms, key chains, posters, and Indian dolls with tiny ski masks and wooden rifles were favorites among political tourists. During the months of February, March, and April, it was common to see masked teens attending rock concerts. At one point it became extremely hard to draw the line between radical politics and pop culture.

Eroticism was a crucial ingredient in Marcos's hype. His soft and sincere voice, and "beautiful hazel eyes" framed by the black mask, turned him into an icon of forbidden sexuality. Many lonesome housewives and starry-eyed students projected their sexual fantasies onto him, writing passionate love letters that were regularly published in national newspapers. Marcos answered each and every one of them. One of his most famous letters, addressed to the writer Elena Poniatowska began with the following line: "Señora, I am prostrate at your feet." In one letter I read in *La Jornada*, an upper-class señora described her desire "to get lost in the jungle with Marcos." In "Los Supermachos," a political cabaret theater piece by Jesusa Rodríguez, a suave Marcos did an incomplete "mask striptease" to the beat of a cumbia. At a transvestite bar in Guadalajara, a Marcos *loca* did a full striptease.

III

Though he has become the most famous Mexican celebrity of 1994, no one knows who he really is. Obsessive discussions about Marcos's "real identity" continue to dominate conversations in homes, at the workplace, in cafés, and in magazines and newspapers. Although deep inside no one wishes to unmask him, every Mexican has a colorful theory about his identity. In one of the early versions he was a foreign intellectual (he speaks fluent English, French, and a few indigenous languages), but soon his Mexico City accent spiced with *norteñismos* caused most to discard that rumor. Many detected traces of liberation theology in his communiqués and interviews, and swore he was a radical Jesuit priest. But the Catholic church vehemently denied this hypothesis. Others perceived him as an ex-leader of the 1968 student movement. But a journalist who spent time with *el Sup* says he is only thirty-eight years old (which means that in 1968 he was a mere thirteen). Other theories have described him as a puppet of a dissident faction within the PRI, a frustrated writer enacting the book he was unable to write, a bisexual hipster, or a mystic propelled by ancient forces who is fulfilling Mayan prophecies that were written in the *Popul Vuh* and *Chilam Balam*. Real-life events have often helped to nurture the version of Marcos as mystic. During the Convención Nacional Democrática [Democratic National Convention] which took place in August in the Chiapaneca village of Aguascalientes, just as Marcos read the last words of his speech, the giant canopy built to protect the six thousand visitors from the elements collapsed on top of them in a sudden, fierce rainstorm.

Fully aware of his mythical dimensions, Marcos has neither denied nor accepted any of these theories. During his many interviews with the press, he has provided very little information about himself. Born "somewhere between the Suchiate River and the Río Bravo" to Spanish immigrant parents, he claims to have spent some time in Northern Mexico, and in the U.S. Southwest, where he says he worked as a waiter in San Francisco and as a taxi driver in Texas. His use of *norteño* slang and his familiarity with Chicano issues make these claims quite probable. According to him, his past ten years were spent in the jungle, training and preparing for the famous upheaval. This is a bit far-fetched for some. "If he was in the jungle all that time," asked Arturo Turok, a photographer who spent time with him during the early days of the insurrection, "how the hell did he obtain his vast knowledge of contemporary world politics and urban culture?"

During the Convención, a very revealing incident occurred. At a press conference, Marcos said that it was time to reveal his identity, and decided to conduct a poll "in the spirit of democracy." He asked how many people would like him to take off his mask, and after a long pause, only two or three raised their hands. Despite the obsessive speculations about his identity, no one really wanted to see his face. To unmask him would strip him of his performance self, crack the myth open, turn him into an ordinary man. This would force him to accept a political defeat, and to abruptly stop his performance. There is, of course, another risk: What if he is ugly or nerdy?

IV

Only an event of epic dimensions can destroy a myth and stop an epic performance. When the tragic assassination of PRI candidate Luis Donaldo Colosio Murrieta occurred in the city of Tijuana (where else could such an event have taken place?), Mexico's attention was drastically diverted, and Marcos moved to Page 2 of the national press. In fear of being blamed for the assassination, the Zapatistas themselves decided to postpone the peace process. Unfortunately, by doing this they lost both momentum and negotiating power. By the time they finally rejected the government proposal meant to appease their rage, Mexico's love affair with Marcos and the romantic indigenous rebels was beginning to fade.

In the month prior to the elections, the same Mexican intelligentsia who had so fervently contributed to Marcos's mystification began to express disenchantment. Carlos Monsiváis was suddenly "fed up with so much hype." Radical political analyst Jorge Castañeda denounced the Zapatistas for "not being part of the democratic process." Other intellectuals began to criticize *La Jornada*'s "romantic and out-dated protrayal of Chiapas," and when the Convención issued invitations to many prominent opposition intellectuals, only a handful responded.

The ultimate paradox is that the fear of Marcos and the EZLN may have contributed to the (re)election of the PRI candidate last August 21. During the electoral media campaign, the PRI made sure to equate change with violence; and to indirectly but firmly suggest that the opposition (any oppositional forces) would bring Mexico the same uncertainty and chaos that inundated the ex–Soviet bloc a couple of years ago. And people swallowed it.

With the vote for no change, Marcos is faced with a very serious predicament. His aura is rapidly losing its shine, his men are being silently besieged by the federal army, their main allies in the PRD are out of the game, and Zedillo, the new president, appears to be even more authoritarian and intransigent than Salinas. It is going to take twice as much performance skill and media savvy for *el Sup* to remain a vital political force.

Many of Marcos's hard-core sympathizers are trying to figure out a dignified exit for the hero. Should he take off the mask in private, go back to his normal self, and disappear for good? Should he commit political suicide or die in time to conquer a space in the Mexican Revolutionary Olympus? Or should he try to become just another important political player in Mexico's opposition; no longer a myth, no longer a performance artist?

As I write this, we still don't know what will happen to Mexico, to the Zapatistas, or to Marcos. It seems that the Zapatista mythology has almost totally evaporated, and the times ahead look very tough. For the moment, all I can say is that there was a time in recent contemporary Mexican history in which we all experimented with the realm of unlimited utopian possibilities. And that these possibilities, as scary or exciting as they may have been for each of us, were partially created by the performance skills of Marcos and the EZLN. As a Mexican writer said, "the Zapatistas achieved in eleven days (of armed activity) what the FMLN was unable to in eleven years"; that is, to determine the terms of the cease-fire, to force the government to sit and negotiate in their own territory, to introduce into the spectrum of Mexican political forces a new vision of the future of the country, and above all, to create a new political mythology in a time when most political mythologies are bankrupt.

"Say no to terrorism. Use Marcondoms against AIDS."

WOMEN, MEXICO, AND CHIAPAS
Elena Poniatowska

AY, WHAT A COUNTRY! ON SEPTEMBER 19, 1985, AT
7:19 A.M., an earthquake devastated Mexico City. More than
twenty thousand people were killed and 100,000 were left home-
less, but the ones who suffered the most were the seamstresses.
Why? Because everyone forgot about them. First, because they
were women and single mothers; second, because they meant
nothing to Mexican society; and third, because they worked in
clandestine factories, sweatshops hidden away in poorly built
structures. It was an atmosphere worthy of Charles Dickens —
nobody is easier to forget than a seamstress.

However haunting the date September 19, 1985, may be for us
Mexicans, it also contains a glimmer of hope; it is the name of a
seamstresses' union, formed in the earthquake's aftermath. It

marks the birth of a new group of women who learned to say, "*Adios, patroncito.*"

Women in Mexico live under the weight of an age-old patriarchy and under a much heavier burden still, that of the Catholic church, which teaches us that life is only a passage and that the meek shall inherit the earth. Although we are only on the earth "for a little while," eternity awaits us in heaven where we will never be hungry, harassed, cheated, beaten, made fun of, and will never beg for money because we will make our own in God's paradise, thanks to His eternal (and economic) compassion.

While they were patiently waiting for the bodies of their companions to be removed from the collapsed buildings, the seamstresses suddenly realized that their boss's main concern was for his safe. They had loved their *patroncito* ["little boss"] because he was so kind and generous as to give them work to do at home. He was the incarnation of man in their lives; the majority had gone from an imaginary father to an imaginary husband. When he went abroad, he brought them holy images and crucifixes from Rome, or keychains and other trinkets from Las Vegas. Now he was weeping over his strongbox and his machinery, ignoring the cries of more than sixty of his buried employees. When the seamstresses went to look for him at home, they were appalled by his huge house, expensive cars, and fancy neighborhood — they who lived in slums. Rage began to grow inside them. "Our *patroncito* is not generous at all, he's a *cabrón*," they discovered. "Just like our government that couldn't care less if we are dead or alive."

Thus was born the September Nineteenth Garment Workers Union, which posed a very female threat to Mexico's corrupt, male-dominated syndicalism. Mexican presidents have the power of God Almighty and the general population tends to kneel in their presence. Nonetheless, women like Evangelina Corona, who did not know how to read or write, stood up in front of former president Miguel de la Madrid, and contradicted him with the innocence of a child. "Oh no, Mr. President, it wasn't at all like you are saying. You have been misinformed. The boss never paid us the last two days of the week. He ran away to Atlantic City with his safe." In a matter of weeks, after burying their companions, or what remained of them (one was identifiable only by the tiny ring on her finger), the women discovered that they deserved to be paid decent wages and receive the same benefits as male workers.

"Twelve-hour workdays, minimal light and ventilation, contracts renewed weekly to discourage troublemakers, supervisors who prevented us from talking to each other on the job, and even followed us to the toilet. We knew little about our legal rights and many of us were single mothers, supporting entire families on $19.00 to $25.00 a week," says Victoria Munive, who has worked in the industry for eighteen years. "Inspectors knew the factories were working illegally, but the factory owners and the government work together, and the inspectors receive bribes to overlook the violations. Higher profits is the owners' only philosophy." She adds, "There were twenty-six women trapped in the building where I worked. More than half were still alive when we got there, but the owners waited for more than two weeks before they started to look for them. By then, of course, it was too late. The women inside didn't have social security, and if you're dead without a card, you never existed at all. No one has to compensate your family for anything. We decided to form a human blockade to halt the indifference."

The first thing to rise from the ashes of Warsaw after the Second World War was a flower shop. Suddenly, an armful of red roses emerged from the rubble. The first thing that came out of the debris in Mexico was a set of rag dolls, made by the seamstresses. With bleeding hands and tears falling onto their aprons, they stitched together little patches of flowery material and made dolls that were designed by Mexican painters. They were exhibited in a museum and later sold to the public, the funds being used to help the surviving seamstresses get back on their feet.

On September 19, 1985, in response to its victims, Mexico City underwent one of the noblest changes of power in its history — the transformation of the people into a government, and of official chaos into civilian order. Democracy, as Carlos Monsiváis points out, can also be the sudden importance of each and every individual.

Contemporary Mexican women, following the example of the seamstresses, are also saying good-bye to their parents, their bosses, their husbands, their confessors, or any form of authority; and privileged women have much to learn from the classes they so despise. The new Mexico (now in crisis) has grown from roots in its poorest states. And now men, women, and children have begun to fight for their rights, with the intelligence and efforts of women like the seamstresses, who came from the streets, or EZLN guerrilleras, who come from the fields of Chiapas.

It's not that there have been *no* women in power in Mexico, but they are the exception that confirms the rule. We have had women governors in the states of Colima and Tlaxcala, and a woman as the head of the House of Representatives. Yet, they can not be considered a factor of change, being part of the official ruling party, the PRI, which has been in power for the last sixty years. However, Ifigenia Martínez, a well-known economist, recently left the PRI to join the PRD (Revolutionary Democratic Party, led by Cuahtémoc Cárdenas). Rosario Ibarra de Piedra, a mother whose son has been missing since 1975, has united peasant women and created a movement against disappearances — that form of political torture which was institutionalized in Argentina and Chile. But the young women of the opposition pose the real challenge, and in 1994, campesinas have risen up and surprised everyone by joining revolutionary forces in the Chiapas jungle. Mexico is a very young country. Forty million — half of the total Mexican population — are minors under the age of seventeen.

January 1, 1994, marked the day that NAFTA was to begin and we were to enter into "modernity" by our own right. On that day, Chiapas, the poorest state in Mexico, suddenly rose up and said, "We, too, are Mexico, and we are not modern. We are illiterate, we have no electricity, no running water, our homes have dirt floors, two-thirds of our children do not have schools, we have the highest tuberculosis rate in the nation, and half of our population does not speak Spanish."

Guerrero, the state where the guerrillas began back in the 1970s, is still in political turmoil — although Acapulco is visited by tourists from all over the world, half the coastal population lacks running water, electricity, and sanitary installations of any kind. Oaxaca, in the south-central region of Mexico, is the origin of the majority of undocumented workers who have gone to seek decent living conditions in the United States.

By starting the Chiapas revolt on January 1st, international press coverage was guaranteed. Twelve days later, beseiged by the clamor of citizens (more than 100,000 marched to the Zócalo chanting: *"Primer Mundo, ¡Já Já Já!"* [First World, Ha Ha Ha!]), His Holiness Salinas, that is, President Carlos Salinas de Gortari, ordered a cease-fire and sent Manuel Camacho Solís to Chiapas to negotiate with the EZLN. But he never anticipated the popularity the Zapatistas would soon gain, and how Subcomandante Marcos — in more than one way — would become a national hero.

Camacho Solís was assisted in his negotiations by a mediator, Bishop Samuel Ruiz García, appointed by the Zapatistas. Why a bishop? Curiously enough, Chiapas is not a religious state, in terms of orthodox Catholicism. On the contrary, the Mayans get drunk and sleep it off on the floor of the church. Beneath the wooden altars and saints made of *maize* are hidden "heathen" idols, which have been worshipped for centuries. At the same time, Protestants have gained great influence among poor Mexican and Guatemalan Indians because they teach them practical things: gardening, health care, garment manufacturing, and cooking. Bishop Samuel Ruiz, allied with the poor, has been accused of practicing liberation theology, instead of following the ideologies traditionally associated with the Vatican. The truth is that the church has been in the forefront of social and political events ever since the conflict began.

Ever since January we live in a new Mexico; the country is in a state of political chaos. In a sea of disaster and desperation, there is a glimmer of hope — in the guise of change — on the horizon. For example, the bottom of the social pyramid, tired of being invisible (like the seamstresses), has been taken into account. Before, we scarcely spoke of misery in our country, and the poor were easily ignored. We got used to seeing little children and their mothers begging in the streets, youngsters, three and four years old, dodging cars while selling Kleenex or chewing gum. It seemed most natural, and the poverty of "the others" became part of daily life — it was our landscape. We were going to enter into NAFTA like Christ with all his beggars and sit happily at the banquet; or was the United States contemplating the inclusion of the indigenous people into the trade agreements? There are more than 6.4 million Indians in our country.

To our surprise, we found out there were Indian women among the leaders of the EZLN in the Lacandón jungle. Women who led battalions and gave orders in a clear, unflinching voice, women called Ramona, Petra, Ana María, Jesusa, Chabela, Amalia. Women who did not know how to read and write and who did not speak Spanish.

More than ten years ago, six men arrived in the Lacandón jungle and said they were there in order to help the peasants rise up in arms. Only after many years, the six became forty, a few women among them. The revolt they launched on the day of NAFTA's implementation focused the eyes of the world on the Zapatistas, who took their name from one of the heroes of the Mexican Revolution, Emiliano Zapata, whose slogan was "*Tierra y Libertad*" [Land and Liberty]. Besides these inalienable (but so often ignored) rights, the EZLN demanded food and housing, education, justice, respect, tractors, water pipes, and, perhaps more than anything else, to be treated like first-class Mexicans and not like the condemned of the earth.

At the same time, in their "Laws of Women," the guerrilleras set down their own rights and demands: no compulsory marriage or unwanted children, and participation in the life of the community, which includes the right to hold political office. They also affirmed their right to study, and even to become truck drivers if they so desire. These laws were subsequently translated into all the indigenous languages of the region, voted on, and approved while their husbands and lovers looked on in fear.

All of them looked like Rigoberta Menchú, except for the fact that they did not wear beautifully embroidered blouses and sashes, nor did they knit ribbons into their thick black braids, but carried two bandoliers of cartridges over their shoulders and a gun strapped onto their hips. These women were hidden away in the muddy trenches in a mountain pass, or behind a red bandana. Anonymous women were leading an army of two thousand Zapatistas.

They communicated with the world through an interpreter, a Mexican who knew Latin and spoke good Spanish, his expressive eyes sparkling with a sense of humor, his speech imaginative, clear, funny, charming, and as far as possible from dull, stern, Marxist jargon. All women (even those belonging to the highest classes) fell in love with him and his extraordinary gaze and hid his picture in their closet, away from the anger of their husband the landowner, the politician, the banker or the lawyer, or the general of the National Armed Forces. Thus, Subcomandante Marcos became famous, so famous that now even condoms wear a ski mask just like his.

Ramona, Ana María, Laura, Marta, and Rocío said they preferred to fight in the war than to die of dysentery, as have more than 177,000 of their community. So they climbed up to the wildest part of the jungle to begin burning bright in the forest of the night, like William Blake's tigers. Like Marcos, they wear masks, but they shy away from interviews because their native tongue is Tzotzil, a Maya language. Ramona and Ana María are nearly bilingual, so they receive journalists and give some answers to the white people's endless barrage of questions.

Lieutenant Amalia tells her story: "My father was a peasant but he learned how to speak Spanish. He's a Ch'ol, and has always been an activist in Chiapas. When I was fifteen, I realized that there was an armed organization in the sierra. I knew how to read and write, but I did not speak Spanish when I entered the army. The army taught me, and in the army I studied Mexican history and combat strategies. It was very hard, but no harder than life at home. When you've carried heavy loads of wood ever since you were ten, everything becomes easy. I am a strong woman. I had never fired a weapon but I found the courage to do it, and to learn how to do it well. My first combat was in Ocosingo. We have arms, but they are not as powerful as those of the national army. Ours are old and beat-up, not modern at all.

"The men here go back home to see their girlfriends and their mothers. I never go back. The army is my family. My compañeros are my brothers and sisters. If two of them want to marry, they have to ask the commander-in-chief. But women must take the pill, because we are not here to take care of babies. If you want a baby, you have to go back to the village. I love being a Zapatista, if not, I would have gone back home long ago. Here, men work in the kitchen and they are not treated like sissies. We don't have much to cook anyway, except for beans, corn, and sometimes coffee.

"Many of us have known Subcomandante Marcos since we were children. In my own home, I don't have much more than what I have here. The same mud hut and the same food. For me, it is preferable to die in combat than to die of cholera or of parasites, so I don't miss the girls at home. I'm called a professional of violence but I don't get any salary."

Just where does the money to support the guerrilla come from? Some have speculated that a major economic contributor could be Ross Perot himself, in a last-ditch attempt to foil the Free Trade Agreement between Mexico, Canada, and the United States. This would not be so surprising, since the United States has consistently provided arms to nearby Central American groups, such as the Contras in Nicaragua and the conservative insurgents of El Salvador.

Finally, let us not forget that ethnically, Chiapas and Guatemala are one.

REVOLUTIONARY WOMEN'S LAW

IN THEIR JUST FIGHT FOR THE LIBERATION OF OUR people, the EZLN incorporates women into the revolutionary struggle regardless of their race, creed, color, or political affiliation, requiring only that they share the demands of the exploited people and that they commit to the laws and regulations of the revolution. In addition, taking into account the situation of the woman worker in Mexico, the revolution supports their just demands for equality and justice in the following Revolutionary Women's Law.

First: Women, regardless of their race, creed, color, or political affiliation, have the right to participate in the revolutionary struggle in a way determined by their desire and ability.

Second: Women have the right to work and receive a fair salary.

Third: Women have the right to decide the number of children they will bear and care for.

Fourth: Women have the right to participate in the affairs of the community and to hold positions of authority if they are freely and democratically elected.

Fifth: Women and their children have the right to primary attention in matters of health and nutrition.

Sixth: Women have the right to education.

Seventh: Women have the right to choose their partner and are not to be forced into marriage.

Eighth: Women shall not be beaten or physically mistreated by their family members or by strangers. Rape and attempted rape will be severely punished.

Ninth: Women will be able to occupy positions of leadership in the organization and to hold military ranks in the revolutionary armed forces.

Tenth: Women will have all the rights and obligations elaborated in the revolutionary laws and regulations.

INTERVIEW: REGIONAL UNION OF CRAFTSWOMEN OF CHIAPAS
Yolanda Castro

J'PAS JOLOVILETIK, OR THE REGIONAL UNION OF Craftswomen of Los Altos de Chiapas, is an organization with 873 members. Soledad runs the store in San Cristóbal de las Casas, where they sell *artesanía* made by the women in the area who belong to their union. Natalia is the union's president, and Yolanda Castro is an adviser.

Natalia and Soledad [pseudonyms they chose to use] come from indigenous communities in Chiapas, and their first language is Tzotzil, a Mayan dialect. The interview was conducted in Spanish. Since Soledad does not speak Spanish, Natalia translated her answers.

How do the indigenous women live in the communities here in Los Altos de Chiapas?

Natalia: Well, the poor women, the way they live now they suffer a lot. They work hard but earn nothing, not like the rich people. They work much harder — carrying wood, working with a machete and hoe — just to feed their children, their families. They never have money. It's not like that for rich people; they don't work so hard.

Soledad: When I was in my community, I got up every day at 4 A.M. to make the tortillas and prepare breakfast. I had to go out to get water, because the community has no running water, so you have to carry it. Then I'd take the sheep out to pasture and on the way back I'd carry wood. When I got back, I would embroider or weave. That's the way the days go, every day. Sometimes I worked with the hoe in the morning, and in the afternoon, I'd grind the corn for tortillas.

You're familiar with the Revolutionary Law of the Zapatista women. Do you agree with their demands?

Yes, we agree.

So you agree that all women should have the right to determine how many children they're going to have?

Natalia: Yes, because it's better.

And they should have the right to choose their own husband, and not be obligated to marry?

Natalia: Yes, because that's how it used to be, we were forced. Sometimes people didn't want to marry off their daughters, but they had to.

How did that work?

Natalia: Well, if a man came to ask for a girl and her parents liked what he brought them, well, then they made their daughter marry him. They think it's better if the girls are married young. Most girls are married at fourteen or fifteen.

When you decided, on your own, to leave your community to come to work with the union in San Cristóbal, what did your family and community think? Did you have problems?

Natalia: My family thought I didn't respect them. I came here against their will, so therefore I didn't respect them anymore. They think that now I can do whatever I want. If I want to be with a lot of men, now I can do it, that's what people say. And for that, they are against me.

And now that you're married and you live with your husband, are they happy?

Well, now they don't care about me; and I don't care about them anymore.

And do the people in your community disapprove of you as well?

Yes, because that's the way it is, they speak badly of people with each other.

So it's difficult for a woman in one of the communities to make the decision to leave and begin working. Do they always look at it this way?

Yes, because they think that women and girls shouldn't decide things for themselves, that daughters should obey. If girls go out alone, then they're not worth anything, because people think bad things about them — that they're out looking for men. Yes, it's like that. . . .

And you, Soledad, what does your family think?

My family and the people in the community say that I don't respect my father, that I came here looking for men. The community is just waiting till I return with a baby. They think that I'll arrive anytime, pregnant, and then they'll laugh at me.

Natalia: The young women don't have the right to leave and work in other places. The custom in the communities is to keep them shut in the house.

There has been talk in the union about the rights of women. What do you think about that?

Natalia: I think it's good. The women are opening up their eyes and beginning to realize that they have rights.

Soledad: I am interested in this, too.

As indigenous women, what is it you would like to ask, or demand of the authorities and the government?

Soledad: They should give us our rights. For example, since we work in *artesanía*, they should pay us a fair price for our work. And we want them to treat us well. Sometimes they treat us very badly and say whatever they want to say to us.

What is it they say?

Natalia: That we're pigs, bums, we don't bathe, things like that. Even now, they still treat us badly. I've even heard that they make fun of the *indígenas* who come to school in their traditional clothes.

Soledad: I studied in Chinalhó. Since I went to school like this, in my traditional Chamula clothes, they made fun of me, saying things like "stupid little Indian," and other things.

And the teachers?

Soledad: The teachers force the children to bathe. And they treat them badly if they don't believe what the teacher is saying. They hit the smaller ones.

Why is it that not all the women in the union participate in the meetings and marches?

Natalia: There are women with their husbands who are in agreement, who want to support, but the men are not accustomed to letting their wives go out. They don't want to take care of the children, or make their own meals. The men are like that. Even though they are in agreement, they don't let the women go.

Does your husband allow you to participate?

Natalia: No.

Soledad: Well, I'm still single, so I can participate. I can do what I want.

Natalia: Women didn't have these rights before. They didn't leave their houses. But when the "problem" started, they began to go out, to participate in marches and meetings.

Soledad: The women are leaving behind their traditions a little, leaving their houses. Now, it's not like it was.

Is it important for you that this has changed? Do the women feel better? Are you hopeful?

Natalia: Well, we're still waiting to see what happens. To see if it gets better, little by little. But I feel good about what is happening right now.

Soledad: Me, too.

We've been threatened, we don't know by whom, exactly. You were here, Soledad, many times when they came looking for me, or came to ask questions. What do you think is going on?

Soledad: Well, it's happened before, they've come looking for you many times. Sometimes they come for me, and it's frightening. They even went to my house, looking for me, asking my full name. And now I feel afraid. I'm afraid to go out in the street because I feel like they're going to grab me, that any minute they could kill me or kidnap me.

And does it make you afraid to participate in marches or meetings?

No.

You want to continue fighting?

Yes, I want to go on. I want to open my eyes more, because it's better. I don't want to stay with my eyes closed, like before.

And you, Natalia, have you been afraid because of all this?

No, the day they came looking for me, I wasn't there. I am not afraid.

What do you think of Subcomandante Marcos?

Natalia: I think what he's doing is good. His work, his will is for a better life for the *indígenas*. He is fighting on our side.

Soledad: Marcos is in favor of the indigenous people. I think it's good, well, we're *indígenas* (laughter).

Chiapas has a long history of rebellion. Is this something new? Has there been anything as important for the indigenous people?

Natalia: Not before this. We didn't know that all this was going to start. If we had rights before this, we didn't know it.

And now that you know, do you think that many people are going to change? Have people changed?

Natalia: Many people have changed. For example, in many of the communities people didn't vote for the PRI; they voted for the PRD. Things have changed now that the people in the communities understand things a bit more.

Did the women vote as well? Did they vote before?

Natalia: Yes, the women voted. Before, they didn't; only the men.

How would things be now if the uprising hadn't happened in January?

Natalia: If this hadn't happened, the rich people would continue to humiliate us. Now they are beginning to have some respect for us, some of them, at least. But there are many who still don't understand, because they are against the indigenous people. They treat us badly. But I see some change now, there is more respect. Because now the *indígenas* know their rights.

How did they come to know their rights?

Natalia: By listening. Only by listening, because there aren't many people who know how to read or write. Most people just heard about it in conversations.

Were there discussions in the communities about rights?

Natalia: I think that this year there is a representative in every community, and they are explaining what's happening. What is good, and what is bad.

Representatives of the EZLN?

Yes, I think so. They bring information about how the talks are going for the Zapatistas.

Do you think that, because of the Zapatistas, things will be better in the future?

Natalia: I think so, but I don't know if it's certain. But yes, I believe they are going to get better. Because before, they didn't let the young girls go out, even to study. Boys, yes, they could go to school. Now it's different, both girls and boys can study. And they see how it is for their parents, that if they don't know how to read or write, they suffer.

EK

INTERVIEW: INDIGENOUS AND CAMPESINO COUNCIL OF CHIAPAS

SAIIC

ONLY TEN DAYS AFTER THE FIRST SHOTS WERE FIRED, every major Indian organization met in San Cristóbal de las Casas to form — along with nonindigenous campesino organizations — the Indigenous and Campesino State Council of Chiapas (CEOIC). The indigenous organizations are in a minority in the tumultuous and fragile coalition. However, they are currently the most active and powerfully vocal faction.

Although the Zapatistas' positions have been minimal in relation to specifically Indian concerns, indigenous organizations throughout the state of Chiapas have taken advantage of the political space opened by the January rebellion to join forces and are developing their own alternative peace proposals. CEOIC has endorsed most of the EZLN's demands; in addition they have called for constitutional reform to enable a new relationship between indigenous peoples and the Mexican state. This would be based in the reorganization of territory, as well as political restructuring. CEOIC proposes the creation of autonomous pluri-ethnic regions which would shift power from the state and the federation to indigenous peoples in the state. Actual geographic regions have not been drawn; territorial demarcation is the next challenge.

Antonio Hernández Cruz is a Tojolabal Indian, founding member and secretary general of the State Indigenous and Campesino Council of Chiapas (ClOAC), which is one of the groups participating in the CEOIC. Following the EZLN uprising, Hernández was among the hundreds of Indians detained and tortured by the military.

Can you tell me what happened to you when you were detained by the military; what did they accuse you of?

We were detained on January 5 until 2:00 P.M. the following day . . . They accused us of being the Zapatistas' political leaders . . . They took us from the car we were riding in, put hoods over our heads and tied them very tightly around our necks. We were like this for twenty-four hours. Then they interrogated us heavily, trying to force us to say that we sympathized or were active in the Zapatista Army. When we said no, they hit us. I received blows in the stomach, chest, back, and head, about twenty hard blows.

Did you denounce this occurrence?

To the national and international press, to the television, but television doesn't report anything. The press didn't report everything that occurred. I have publicly denounced the detention in meetings but the only thing which remains is the message, no actions have been taken. After being freed, I vomited blood for two days, because the beatings were severe. The hoods they put on us had ground chili pepper and our eyes were stinging. The powder would fall in our eyes with the slightest movements, and also we were tied up.

Do you think torture has become common?

What was done to us was humanitarian compared to what they did to other compañeros. People are tortured simply because they do not speak Spanish very well, and do not understand orders they are given. From the maximum security cell where they held us, you could hear the beatings and continuous screams.

In addition to being repressive, is the military fearful of what could happen with the Zapatista revolt?

Absolutely. When they had us in the jail cell, we noticed that even though we were tied up, they came to look for us in groups of seven or ten people and would point their guns at us. They were afraid of the people they were holding. I imagine that if we were fighting in the jungle, and armed, that it would be more difficult for them.

Regarding the past events, we do not know if this conflict can be resolved or not. We as organizations have taken the initiative; in order to come to an understanding with national society, there will have to be profound reforms to establish a new relationship between the indigenous communities, society as a whole, and the government.

What type of reforms does the State Council have in mind?

We have been advancing in the attempt to establish a comprehensive plan for indigenous peoples' rights. We need constitutional reform where a whole new chapter establishes various articles that speak of Indian peoples' concrete rights.

Do the peoples in Chiapas speak their own languages or have they stopped speaking them?

Many people have stopped speaking them, because they think that their language is inferior to the other society's. They have been raised to believe this way. There are moments when we are dominated, and then we stop speaking our language.

Is this still occurring or are there now processes to recover these languages?

Now, there is more awareness of our identity. Many people now — even those that are not Indians — call themselves Indian peoples. The consciousness of the indigenous people is much greater than it was two or three years ago. Now with this situation, it's accelerated even more.

Why do you think the struggle in Chiapas appears more like a campesino rather than an Indian struggle?

Definitively because of the negation of indigenous culture. We are discounted and in discounting us they say that we are backward, inferior to the other society. For this reason, many brothers refuse to tell the truth that they are Indian. That is why the struggle is known more as a campesino movement and we are seen as campesinos; nothing more than campesinos.

What is occurring with the supposed progressive allies? How do they see you?

Well, there are many allies that have begun to understand, little by little, as we talk. As they become more aware, they are surprised that we are not inferior, but that we have our own capabilities, our own culture, and our own identity. Now we are organizing at the level of both campesino and indigenous, under the principle of mutual respect. The intellectuals, the students, the allies are all surprised that we are more than they imagined.

When you raised demands for self-governance and autonomy, did you encounter any type of resistance to these ideas?

There are still many problems with the process we are undertaking. With the appearance of the EZLN, we need to accelerate this process even more. At the same time, there are problems with Protestant sects in the communities; with *caciques* who impose their way of life on our communities. These are the problems and difficulties that are present in the indigenous communities.

Do most of these sects negate indigenous peoples' rights to self-governance?

Yes, the Catholic church has taken on a new understanding with the indigenous communities and has proposed that we be recognized by the Constitution. On the other hand, although they have not openly stated it, the other religions are, in practice, trying to totally exterminate us as peoples.

Have the Maya preserved their spirituality, or has it become mixed with Catholicism?

There is a mix, but the Maya religion is present. Our elders tell us that our great ruler the Sun is one of the great gods on this earth, and that our mother is the Earth, that is how we understand everything. The Mayan calendar is also known a little but is no longer used in the Mayan religion . . .

What percentage of indigenous people have land in Chiapas? Do they have enough?

It's difficult in concrete terms to give you a number of people that have land and those that don't. Approximately 60 percent have land, and the other 40 percent are still peons working for landowners.

Do they have enough land to live on?

Those who have been awarded land [in agrarian reforms] have an average of five hectares per person. These lands, however, are in the mountains and of poor quality, while the bottomlands are held by landlords . . .

How have the landlords displaced the indigenous people from their lands? Was it before or after the revolution in Chiapas?

Here in Chiapas we have been organizing the revolution since independent organizations, like ours, started; it dates back twenty to thirty years. At that time, indigenous people began to recover the lands that were ours. We began what the government calls "land invasions," but we were only recovering lands which were ours. The years 1979 and 1980, until 1985, were some of the most difficult for us, because the government displaced us from our lands. They disappeared people, killed our leaders, in short, the government carried out heavy repression against the communities, because we had begun to recover lands which were taken from us by the landlords. This primarily occurred in the north, cases such as those of Simojovel, Huichipan, Bochil, and Nuevo Pueblo.

When did the aggression against the Mayan people begin? It isn't new is it?

Definitely not, we have been suppressed in a thousand ways. We have been brutally repressed, like any animal, for many years. Some periods were especially acute due to the policies applied by the governors of Chiapas.

In regard to the January 1st uprising, did it surprise you?

There were some signs, but I believe that the Zapatistas knew how to prepare this movement very discretely, because they didn't give much information, they didn't give concrete numbers. In our organization we have said that we don't accept, at this time, the armed struggle. Nonetheless many of our brothers felt that there was no other way, that the anger had become too great, that is why the Zapatista army appeared.

The Zapatista communiqués do not talk much about indigenous rights. As indigenous people, what points do you have in common with the Zapatistas?

We believe that the advances made by the Zapatistas are part of the proposal. We are completing the proposal's political and ideological parts for new restructuring of territories and the national political structure.

Do you think that the Zapatistas will accept this?

I think they will. They are making demands for these proposals seriously and will make them part of their program.

Is the change to Article 27, eliminating community property, negative for indigenous people?

It is completely negative. In the end it is the weapon that will destroy our people, because it is a way of dividing us into pieces, families or individuals, because the lands will be privatized. In the *ejidos* everyone will have their parcel, with title to their property, and the collective life of the community will be destroyed.

Have you considered the problems that have been created in the communities as a result of the clashes between the Zapatistas and the military?

Many times these problems are natural because many communities are governed by indigenous and nonindigenous *caciques* who accuse people of being Zapatistas even if they aren't. The mayors and the *caciques* have taken advantage of the moment to try and exterminate our companions in the communities that are forging a new path for national democracy.

Do you feel that indigenous continental unity is important?

Definitely, the indigenous international network is part of the struggle. It is our support and protection. That is the case with this war in Chiapas. These movements are necessary.

LAND AND INDIGENOUS COSMOVISION

Neyra P. Alvarado Solís

IN ORDER TO FULLY UNDERSTAND THE INDIGENOUS peoples' struggle for land, it is fundamental to consider the mystical relationships that indigenous societies establish with it. The armed uprising in Chiapas awakened consciousness of this issue. The Zapatistas' demands are legitimate for all of the diverse indigenous communities of Mexico, who have lived in historic injustice. Nevertheless, the beauty and substance of their cosmovisions have left an imprint, and continue to enrich the life of the country.

In Mexico today, there are officially fifty-six ethnic groups; within these can be found a linguistic and cultural variety which far exceeds that number. The cosmovision of each group expresses a regional and communal reality, elaborated through history. These are agrarian cultures where land is life, sustained by relationships with supernatural forces, and nurtured in communal and familial rituals, depending on good weather and on ritual actions to continue the annual cycle of existence.

In their rituals, fears, uncertainties, and desires are expressed in a constant prayer for life. Corn carries an extraordinary symbolic weight, evident in the culinary arts and in the social and ritual structures that are considered indissoluble aspects of human integrity. Plants, the weather, the land, animals, water, and the stars — observed and apprehended in the natural world — all constitute essential elements of the cosmovision.

Land is an essential part of being, and is worked, cared for, and ritualized in this context. The various ruptures that indigenous people have suffered with the land — whether by extensive and technologized agriculture, large ranches, or the exploitation of forests — have led to the disintegration and isolation of their communities. This erosion and the influx of consumer goods have caused seasonal — sometimes permanent — migrations to areas of intensive agriculture, to manufacturing regions, or even to other countries in search of employment.

All of this has, in some cases, led them to organize to defend their vital living space — the land.

The Mexicaneros of Durango

The Mexicaneros inhabit an area along the borders of Durango, Nayarit, Jalisco, and Zacatecas. They share the interethnic region with Huicholes, Coras, and Tepehuanos, but have remained largely unknown, having historically been a minority in relation to these other groups. They speak a dialect of Náhuatl.

The Mexicaneros are farmers, growing primarily corn, beans, and squash. In the dry season, the young men and their families migrate to the coast of Nayarit to work as agricultural day-laborers, gathering tobacco or cutting sugar cane. They return to their communities to prepare the land for sowing, the harvest, and for the ceremonies connected to the agricultural cycle. These ceremonies are called *xuravét*, a Cora term that means "great star."

For the Mexicaneros, the earth, sun, land, water, deer, Jesus, fire, and the morning star are all deities to be paid homage. The *xuravét*, or "custom" takes place three times a year: the prayer for rain in April or May; the blessing of the corn in September or October; and the thanksgiving for the harvest in January or February. During the ceremony, they ask for health, rain, and good harvests: life. Offerings to the Sun and to fire — deer, and the fruits of the earth and their labor — are an exchange of gifts with the gods who provide for their existence.

For the Mexicaneros, the armed movement of the indigenous communities of Chiapas was born in a reality that they also are living. They support them, and grieve for the loss of life. They are aware of the Zapatistas' demands, and know why they are fighting; the news that comes to them is varied, but the struggle for land and life is legitimate. A Mexicanero says, "We can't help them to struggle with rifles, but we support them, and through the *xuravét* we pray for them. We pray for the war to end, for us all to be able to live on our land with our families, as we have the right to do in this life in which Our Eternal Parents have left us. We are all tired of the injustices, and we all struggle in our own ways to survive."

CR

LAND

IN CHIAPAS, 58.3 PERCENT OF THE WORKING POPU-
lation is in the agricultural sector, where traditional farming
practices, with insufficient modernization and little crop diver-
sification, prevail (*El Financiero*, January 5, 1994).

For decades, the region's economy was based on coffee,
wood, cattle, and corn, but production has declined dramatically over the past five years. In 1989, the imposition of a ban
on forestry removed a source of income for the region's inhabitants. The international price of coffee fell from $120 to 140 to
an average of $60 to 70 per 100 pounds, leading to a 65 percent
decrease in producers' incomes. The closure of the govern-
ment-controlled Inmecafé company eliminated channels of
commercialization and technical support in the region. Cattle-
breeding experienced a crisis of profitability, while corn productivity fell as a result of the exhaustion of available land (Luis
Hernández Navarro in *La Jornada*, January 9, 1994).

The fight for land tenure has been a source of tension in the
state throughout its history. Since the beginning of this century, the region's cattle ranchers and farm owners have been
accused of depriving the Indians of their lands, through violence and threats, with the protection of local governments.
Chiapas is the state with the second largest number of *ejidos*
and agrarian communities in the country, with a total of 2,072,
as well as being the state with the highest number of campesino
takeovers of private farming land. There is also the pressure of
overpopulation. From 1980 to 1990, Chiapas reported an average growth rate of 5.4 percent annually, twice the average

annual rate for the whole country, which was 2.15 percent during the same period (Sergio Sarmiento in *El Financiero*, January 24, 1994).

INTERVIEW: EMILIANO ZAPATA CAMPESINO ORGANIZATION

Vivian Newdick

THE EMILIANO ZAPATA CAMPESINO ORGANIZA-tion [Organización Campesina Emiliano Zapata - Coordinación Nacional Plan de Ayala] has been engaged in land struggles of indigenous and non-indigenous people throughout Chiapas for fourteen years. The leader who was interviewed preferred to remain anonymous, citing an organizational philosophy of group effort over individual identity. He begins:

The struggle for land is fundamental. Our goal is not only to obtain land, but also to increase productivity in the countryside and to create a market for the commercialization of our products, with the participation of all the communities and ethnic groups in political life, both in the state of Chiapas and in the rest of the country.

We believe there have been changes lately, there has been an opening. We don't want war, we're not in agreement with the war. We think that progress toward democracy, toward freedom, can't be won with arms. But to be peacefully won, there has to be space for social and state organizations and for civil society to participate in the construction of democracy. It must come from below, from the communities.

Your organization has been working for fourteen years; these are things that you have proposed from the start, aren't they?

Yes, this has been our struggle for a long time. Since the organization was founded, the fundamental objective was land for the campesinos, for the people who worked the land. For example, right now we're dealing with a law that was passed when Patrocinio Gonzalez was governor of Chiapas that prohibits cutting wood in the forest. This law affected the communities in the region a great deal because many compañeros make their living from wood. From coal, mainly, from the natural products. It's not true that when they passed that law they stopped deforestation; it goes on. It's not possible to save the life of a tree and deny the life of the people in the indigenous communities. That did a lot of damage. The struggle for better living conditions in this state has to do with *all* of the natural resources.

We think that land is a fundamental problem, but at the same time, there is no justice. And lack of education is also a fundamental problem.

How has the organization been changed by what happened on January 1st?

To us, what happened was nothing strange. The violence in this state, assassinations, this had all been going on for a long time. We've had twenty-two of our members killed, including our compañero Arturo Alvarez Velazco, who was our leader and who lives on in the struggle.

Before January 1st, it was a very difficult period, with division between organizations and repression by the state. There was no freedom, people were oppressed and were being displaced from their land. When the EZLN surfaced it shook Mexico, and you could say it changed the world's perspective. The world came to know the other face of Mexico, the poverty, marginalization, oppression, and violence in this country. And it was made clear that neoliberal politics are a disaster, the whole neoliberal project and its programs, like the so-called Solidarity Program — their "support" which never made it to the communities. The war *is* its failure. Twelve days after war was declared, the compañeros in the EZLN declared a cease-fire to give civil society a chance to participate in the democratization of the state. The people made it clear that they didn't want a war, and the EZLN let them have their way. But if there are changes now, it's because the space was created.

Since January 1st, the organizations have played a very important role in the democratization process. We are beginning a new era; we're in a new stage of organizing and there is a very concerted regional integration taking place. The organizations are growing, and the level of consciousness has been elevated. Because the people understand that our brothers in the EZLN rose up in arms for land, education, services, health, and housing, for freedom and human rights — it's what people have been asking for all along. And now there is a space for participation.

People have woken up, but not to say, "Fine, we've arrived at a higher level of consciousness, let's go to war." The communities are clear that it's only by becoming organized and united that we're going to be able to avoid a war. To achieve the fundamental goals — peace, an opening that permits us to achieve democracy, justice, and freedom of speech — we, the organizations, have to direct civil society, and so we play an important role at this moment.

We have left war behind, but that doesn't mean there is peace in Chiapas. Yes, the EZLN has stepped aside to make space for civil society to step in, but the EZLN has not given up its arms.

Part of the struggle is land takeovers, right?

Part, but not all. We are fighting against the revision of Article 27. The new Article 27 does not protect communal property in any way, instead it protects private property at the expense of communal property. Now you can sell the land, or rent it, or give it away as a gift. But not if you have debts — with this new law, if you are indebted they can take everything, you have no option to be paid anything. This is part of the fight for the land as well.

What significance does the indigenous makeup of the EZLN have to the overall struggle in Chiapas?

Clearly the EZLN is made up, in its majority, of indigenous people who have been oppressed. But we think that the part of Chiapan society which does not speak its own language have been even more oppressed, because they've been dispossessed not only of their land, but also of their culture — their language — which is more than what has happened to the compañeros in the EZLN. They speak their own languages, there are still entire regions where they speak these languages. We have been dispossessed of everything. We live in conditions which are more desperate still, because in addition to killing our grandfathers and fathers, they stole our language. Of course, our historic roots are alive and that is our hope. We believe the trunk is still alive, and will sprout new branches. And that's why the repression has been so strong, why they prohibit freedom and participation in politics for the society, the people.

How do the campesino organizations work with the EZLN? What roles do they play?

We don't work together, or rather, our struggle is different. We are not armed, nor do we want to be. We want to participate as a part of civil society, and that is the difference from the EZLN, regarding the roles we play. They're not giving us arms, but they enable us to better realize our work, because civil society will be less repressed. And although we don't agree with their method of struggle, we are brothers — theoretically and historically — and that is precisely what unites us. We have the same objectives, but different methods. The struggle unites us, the struggle for land and freedom, and the struggle of organizations for the space to participate.

And for you, personally, what is the EZLN?

Their role is very important at this moment of the struggle; their function is a historic defense of the people.

And in terms of the five hundred years of struggle, what role do they have?

In all the long history of the struggle which the indigenous people have been waging for five hundred years — the resistance — they have never managed to kill us. They've tried to finish us off, but they have never done it. A moment ago, I said they killed our cultures, our fathers, a certain part of the trunk, but the root remains and it's still green. It's been mixed, of course, but that root is what is conserved today in the struggle of the people, in the fight to recover some, or all, of what belonged to us.

The EZLN are indigenous people who are not fighting for something they don't have any right to. As far as their methods, there was a time when the Indians defended themselves with spears, with arrows, in various ways. In my view, the EZLN's more sophisticated weapons, beyond arming them, do social work. What motivates them isn't the arms, what wins them the respect of the government isn't weapons, it's the work that the compañeros have been doing for many years in this region, the consciousness-raising. They are not in favor of arms either, nor do they want a war. They're fighting in order to avoid a war. They are at war against war, and the most important thing for them is the participation of civil society.

Many people in the United States are going to see this book. Is there anything you would like to say to them?

First, for our indigenous brothers in other countries, although we are not there with you, fight on for the rights of the Indios, for recognition.

Part of our struggle is to liberate a part of our society, to obtain the participation of indigenous people in the political life of our country. We have had no voice, no word. Those who are struggling for that which belongs to them, though they are in other countries, are our comrades. We would like it if when those compañeros read this, they know that they are not alone — that our struggle is not only Mexico, not only Chiapas, and it's not the beginning, because they have already begun.

We have not forgotten the historic struggle of the indigenous peoples, our ancestors, our grandfathers, our brothers. The struggle is for everyone, for nonindigenous people as well. For the people who have no voice. Our fight is their fight.

EK

STATEMENT OF SUPPORT
Leonard Peltier

— on the occasion of the first visit to the
United States by representatives of the EZLN

DEAR SISTERS AND BROTHERS,

Even though I am incarcerated at Leavenworth Prison, and
have been for the past eighteen years, the courageous struggle of
the people of Chiapas and Mexico has reached us here.

We, the indigenous people of North America know very well
the circumstances of our sisters and brothers in Mexico. We too
have the highest infant mortality and the lowest income; we live
either on unproductive, dry land or on reservation land desired
by mining, oil, mineral, gas, or hotel corporations; our lands are
used as dump sites for toxic wastes. Three-quarters of all Indian
land has been stolen from us; our mountains and sacred places
have been defiled; our children stolen from us, and our language
as well.

Your struggle, which was so magnificently brought to world attention on January 1st is an inspiration to all of us. Your blood is our blood. Your fight is our fight. Your victory is our victory.

I am a Lakota native man. I have not seen my home for eighteen years. I have been falsely accused of shooting two FBI agents on Indian land, at the Pine Ridge reservation in 1974. Even though millions of people have signed petitions for my release; even though evidence has been uncovered stating that the FBI had no idea who killed their agents; and even though a campaign for pardon has been launched by my defense committee, which has fought for my freedom these many years, I am still jailed by the U.S. government. The same U.S. government that has imposed NAFTA on your country and mine; the same U.S. government that has supported the Salinas government these many years; the same U.S. government that allows U.S. corporations to exploit Mexican people.

I welcome the representatives of the EZLN to what is, in truth, my country. I hope your visit here will inspire my people and others. I offer my handshake in solidarity with your great struggle. May victory be yours.

In the spirit of Crazy Horse,
Leonard Peltier, political prisoner

A NORTH AMERICAN INDIGENIST VIEW
Ward Churchill

> When the EZLN was only a shadow, creeping through the mist
> and darkness of the jungle, when the words "justice," "liberty," and
> "democracy" were only that: words; barely a dream that the elders of
> our communities, true guardians of the words of our dead ancestors,
> had given us in the moment when day gives way to night, when hatred
> and fear began to grow in our hearts, when there was nothing but
> desperation; when the times repeated themselves, with no way out,
> with no door, no tomorrow, when all was injustice, as it was, the true
> [people] spoke, the faceless ones, the ones who go by night, the ones
> who are in the jungle.
>
> — *EZLN Communiqué*

I HAVE BEEN ASKED TO ADDRESS A FEW REMARKS to the meaning of the recent armed insurrection of the EZLN (or "Zapatistas," as they are popularly known) in Chiapas, Mexico. I am happy to do so because the Chiapas revolt is something I take to hold a genuinely profound significance. Before beginning, however, I think it's important to note that I possess no special knowledge of or relationship to the Zapatistas. The same holds true with regard to the so-called "Lacandón Maya" communities — actually, there are five distinct groups which are often erroneously lumped together under this rubric: Tzotziles in the highlands, Tzeltales and Tojolabales at lower elevations, and Ch'oles and Ch'oltis down in the flatlands — from whence the Zapatista fighters come.[1]

My basis for speaking to the matter at all derives, I suppose, from my having spent the past dozen or so years involved in articulating essentially the same *indigenista* politics by which the EZLN professes itself to be guided; that, and the fact that I have been a participant in the overall struggle, including some aspects of the armed struggle, to realize these politics on behalf of indigenous peoples the world over. So it's from a fairly general perspective of commonality, affinity, and solidarity, not from a position of directly shared experience or "insider" status, that I'll try and contextualize the situation in Chiapas. I think it's both appropriate and necessary to do this because what is happening in southern Mexico is by no means an isolated phenomenon. To the contrary, I see it as part of a far broader process which may in many ways come to redefine the sociopolitical and economic landscape over the years ahead.

With that said, maybe the place to start is with the observation that the Zapatistas have clearly endeavored to place themselves within the whole sweep of American Indian resistance to colonial domination which has been ongoing without real interruption since the first conquistador set foot in this hemisphere more than five hundred years ago.[2] There are many ways of apprehending the intent of the EZLN to make this linkage, but, most obviously, it is signified in the organization's choice to identify itself with the name and spirit of Emiliano Zapata, undoubtedly the revolutionary figure in Mexico who is most closely associated with the historical assertion of native rights in that country. As the matter has been put elsewhere, "In the storehouse of Mexico's political heroes, Zapata becomes for [Indians] the nationalist hero of indigenous rights, a kind of post-revolutionary 'saint,' a Bartolomé de Las Casas of this century, with a gun."[3]

For those who don't know, and I suspect there are some who don't, Zapata was himself an Indian — a Zapoteca, if I remember correctly — from the state of Morelos, to the west of Mexico City. During the Mexican Revolution of 1910–1917, he forged a powerful army composed mainly of other Indians and played a crucial role in bringing the rebels to power. All the while, his position, which he advanced quite strongly, was that in post-revolutionary Mexico the rights to land and political liberty of Indians should be accorded the same dignity and respect as those of any other social or economic sector of the population. For this, he was assassinated in the aftermath of victory by his ostensible comrades-in-arms — the PRI's non-Indian leadership — because his notion that Indians possess such fundamental rights did not fit into their plans to "modernize" the Mexican state.[4]

Insofar as the PRI turned out to be just as bad as previous regimes, and in some ways even worse in terms of Indian interests, Zapata's unflinching stance on behalf of his people, and the fate he suffered as a result, has converted him into something of an icon among those who feel that Indians have been and continue to be wronged by Mexico's postrevolutionary governments.[5] It is therefore both natural and appropriate that the EZLN seized upon the image of Zapata as its primary means of projecting itself to the broader public. One might even describe their appropriation of Zapata's legacy, whether real or imagined, as a media coup of the first order.

I would argue, however, that bound up in the insurgents' rhetoric of self-characterization is something which goes well beyond the embrace of a given moment, personality, or impulse of twentieth-century Mexican revolutionary politics, no matter how important these may have been — or continue to be — in their own right. This devolves first and foremost, I think, on the desire of the Zapatistas to reclaim their own tradition, that of the Maya — virtually the entire composition of the EZLN is Mayan, after all — from the systematic misrepresentation and negation it has suffered at the hands of eurocentric scholarship and other forms of colonialist propaganda. The point probably sounds much too abstract when framed this way, so let me break it down a bit.

As many of you are perhaps aware, the Maya are typically presented by "conventional" anthropology and historiography as such as being "naturally placid," even "docile."[6] If, by this, it were meant that they were/are simply a peaceful people, or amalgam of peoples, the description would be rather stupid and derogatory in its word choices, but nonetheless accurate to a considerable degree. What is meant to be conveyed in the depiction, however, is nothing so backhandedly positive. Instead, what is fostered is the idea that the Maya are basically unwilling or unable to defend themselves against whatever ravages the dominant society may wish to inflict upon them, that they are by individual temperament and cultural disposition malleable, abusable, exploitable, and ultimately expendable whenever their colonizers deem it expedient — usually for reasons of profitability — to liquidate them in whole or in part.[7]

There is of course a code imbedded in this supposedly "balanced, objective and scientific" portrayal of the Maya, the crux of which is that being Mayan equates to being little more than a "natural victim" of the colonizers who have overrun, or who are even now overrunning you, obliterating your way of life for their own purposes, appropriating all that is rightly yours for their own benefit, killing you and yours to suit their fancy. For the members of the colonizing culture itself, the message is one of authorization and validation: that it is not only permissible but natural and inevitable to victimize the Maya in more-or-less any way one sees fit, so long as "progress" — this is the euphemism used to encompass all forms of material gain accruing to the colonizing society — is served.[8]

For the Maya — and it is important to note that, through

such modes as missionarization/Christianization and, to some extent, the "public education system" and mass media, the Maya like other indigenous peoples have been increasingly indoctrinated with the same mythologies about themselves which have been inculcated among their colonizers — there are also messages: "Indianness" and victimization are synonymous; to be a victim of colonial oppression is therefore both your heritage and your destiny; to be truly consistent with yourself you must not only acquiesce in what is done to you by your oppressors, you must — at least if you are to be prideful of your tradition — comport yourself in ways which facilitate their activities at your expense.[9] The psychological matrix of conditioning inherent to advanced colonialism is thus seamless and complete: both colonizer and colonized are assigned their proper roles in perpetuating and perfecting the structure of colonial relations.[10]

What the Zapatistas have set out to do, at least in part, is to kick a very big hole in the imperial paradigm. This is by way, first of all, of organizing themselves in a manner — that of an effective politico-military formation — of which the Mayas have long been said by colonialism's experts on the topic to be inherently incapable. And they have done it the hard way, creating a stable fighting force of about eight thousand before initiating hostilities (this is as compared to the fifteen to twenty thousand fielded by the FMLN in El Salvador at its peak). As the Mexican analyst Arturo Santamaría Gómez has observed:

> The Zapatistas are not *foquistas* [in the manner of Che Guevara]; they do not advocate founding a small nucleus of armed fighters with the expectation of growing in the course of confrontations with the state. They appear to have followed a strategy of the "cold accumulation of forces," which was previously used by the Revolutionary Organization of the People in Arms (ORPA) in Guatemala. ORPA, which is now part of the National Revolutionary Unity of Guatemala (URNG) was founded in 1972 . . . and spent "seven long years of silent work" . . . developing a guerrilla organization, one which was also made up largely of [Mayas].[11]

Second, they have successfully engaged that organization against the Mexican military in the provincial cities of San Cristóbal and Ocosingo; another impossibility, according to "the experts." This separates the EZLN quite dramatically from other contemporary guerrilla efforts in Mexico, such as those undertaken by the non-Indians of the National Revolutionary Civic Association (ACNR) and the Party of the Poor (PP) between 1967 and 1974. As Santamaría Gómez has noted, the "Zapatistas constitute a novel type of armed political movement. They can be clearly distinguished from previous guerrillas in Mexico, as well as elsewhere in Latin America, in terms of their ideas and military practices."[12] The results tend to speak for themselves:

> The uprising led by the EZLN is much larger, better planned and more extensive geographically than any other in recent times. The ACNR and the PP [which could muster only fifty and two hundred fighters, respectively] were never in a position to consider taking over cities the size of San Cristóbal (population roughly eighty thousand) or Ocosingo (about 100,000).[13]

All of this takes us to the point I'm trying to make here, they have managed to do these things in such a way as to tie them into the *real* history and tradition of the Maya rather than the racist and self-serving falsification of that tradition contrived by academic minions of the colonial status quo.[14] The Zapatista method of organizing and fighting is consciously and unequivocally Mayan at every level:

> In another break with the traditional model of guerrilla insurgency, the EZLN has apparently rejected the idea of leadership by a single, charismatic *caudillo*. In the early days of the insurrection, the government appeared intent on creating a principal leader by singling out the commander of the EZLN's military operation in San Cristóbal de Las Casas, Subcomandante Marcos [one of the very few non-Maya fighters]. However, both Marcos and other representatives of the Zapatistas speak of a "committee" which makes decisions, rather than any individual.[15]

It turns out that this committee — "council" would probably be a better term — is comprised of representatives selected for that purpose by the residents of the individual villages that have committed fighters to the struggle. It is this form of military administration and decision making, a form which plainly incorporates elements of the participatory manner of Mayan governance — a distinctly different proposition from other known revolutionary styles of command, Zapata's included — which allows the EZLN to maintain that "it is not a group of guerrillas but a regular army" representing a nation in its own right.[16] And this in turn is what most obviously ties the Zapatistas back, not to Zapata and the Mexican Revolution, but to Mayan tradition itself.

How and why? The answers lie squarely in those actualities of post-invasion Mayan history which the colonial intelligentsia has been most anxious to obfuscate or dissolve. To take an example from very early on, the Mayas of the northern Guatemalan highlands — the locale immediately south of Chiapas — organized themselves on the same village-by-village basis as the Zapatistas. When the army they put together went on the offensive during the 1630s it possessed sufficient force to drive the recently-arrived Spanish completely out of the area. It took nearly half a century before effective colonial rule could be reestablished in the area.[17] There are a number of other examples I could use to illustrate the theme — about twenty, if memory serves, none of them on the scale of the seventeenth-century rising, but all of them effective in their way — the point is that the Mayan tradition is the exact opposite of what is taught in school or printed in the newspapers. Far from being passive in the face of colonial domination, the Mayas have been fighting back with every means at their disposal for the past 350 years.[18] And — witness the EZLN — their struggle is very much alive today.

Now it may be that all of this is a sort of "back-channel" communication, of exemplary action being used by a certain group of Mayas to talk to other Mayas about the nature of Mayan culture and tradition. To some extent that must be true since such emic discourse is always an integral aspect of intellectual decolonization.[19] The advantage to non-Mayas in seeking to penetrate the veil of popularized Zapata imagery with which the EZLN has thus far shrouded its inner dynamics is that it allows for a much better apprehension of the magnitude of the alternative manifested in the Chiapas revolt. Like it or not, Emiliano Zapata was firmly wedded to the overall complex of goals, aspirations, and attitudes marking the Mexican Revolution. Consequently, although he was martyred by it, his legacy can never be entirely divorced from the drive to consolidate the modern Mexican nation-state, an entity of the very sort which is most antithetical to native self-determination.[20]

The whole history of Mayan resistance, on the other hand, links itself to the exact opposite, to the native struggle against the emergence and eventual hegemony of such states in this hemisphere. Put another way, the Mayan tradition represents an undeviating and unextinished refusal of indigenous peoples to abdicate their inherent rights to organize themselves socially, culturally, and spiritually, to develop and maintain their own forms of economy, to regulate and govern themselves, and control the resources within their own territories; in a word, the assertion of national sovereignty.[21] Self-evidently, the motivations incorporated into this sort of "sovereigntist" or "ethnonationalist" outlook add up to something very different from those at play when the objective of insurgency is to achieve a transformation allowing a greater degree of sociopolitical and economic equity among groups *within* some overarching statist structure such as Mexico.[22]

At this level, I can only conclude that the Zapatista agenda must be sharply differentiated from that of the Mexican revolutionaries, including Zapata, just as it should from the objectives espoused by Marxian figures such as Che Guevara, Salvador Allende, Raul Sendic, and Fidel Castro or the Sandinistas, Tupamaros, Sendero Luminoso, M-19, FMLN, and other leftist guerrilla organizations.[23] Instead, the EZLN should be viewed, through its deliberate internal alignment with the spirit of the 1630 Mayan revolt, as joining — conceptually and emotionally — the much broader historical stream of indigenous resistance in the Americas: that of the Manaus led by Ajuricaba in Brazil during the mid-1700s, for example,[24] or the Incan revolt headed by Túpac Amaru in the Andean highlands in 1780,[25] or the Araucaño fighters in Argentina and the Mapuche revolt in Chile during the 1870s and 1880s.[26] And then again there is the inspiration of the armed struggle of the Yaquis to maintain their Sonoran homeland free from Mexican domination, an effort that lasted well into the twentieth century, and which to this day has never been truly abandoned.[27]

Nor is there reason to stop at the Río Grande. The magic line dividing Ibero from Anglo America is something contrived for the convenience of Euroamerican colonizers, an arrangement among themselves; it has nothing at all to do with the inter-associative traditions of American Indians. Hence, the Zapatista phenomenon is as much an extension of the resistance of Powhatan or Pontiac to British imperialism as it is of the example of Túpac Amaru or Ajuricaba.[28] It has as much to do with the 1680 Pueblo Revolt as with that of the Mayas a half-century before, as much to do with Tecumseh's confederation as with the Yaquis, as much to do with Roman Nose's Cheyenne Dog Soldiers as with the Araucaño resistance, as much to do with Sitting Bull, Gall, Crazy Horse, and the other Lakotas who destroyed Custer as with the Mapuches.[29] And, to be sure, there are many others who might be mentioned, both north and south of the river: Captain Jack, Seattle, Cochise and Geronimo, Satanta and Satank, Louis Riel, Almighty Voice, Quannah Parker, Hugo Blanco, Little Crow, the Redsticks, Osceola, John Ross and Nancy Ward; the list goes on and on.

I submit to you that *this* is the foundation upon which the EZLN is building its actions, actions which are in some ways otherwise inexplicable. Theirs is a perspective developed and tempered in a worldview which is emphatically indigenous, not one that has been skewed into conformity with one or another variant of Marxist or neo-Marxist doctrine. One suspects this will remain the case regardless of how many non-Indian university professors or students such as Subcomandante Marcos are incorporated into the ranks of the Zapatistas to act as liaisons to the "outer world," and why, as Salvador Castañeda, a former guerrillero and current director of the Center for Investigations of Armed Movements, has put it, the EZLN insurgents demonstrate "an original conception of popular warfare [and] great support from the [native] population."[30]

Obviously, there are many dimensions to this "Indianness" or, more accurately, *indigenismo*, discerned by Castañeda. I have touched upon only one aspect, that of resistance, in my commentary. In order to be thorough, it would be necessary to go into the nature of the spiritual grounding evident among Zapatista fighters,[31] the atypicality — from the standpoint of most insurgent theory and practice — of the concern they manifest with regard to ecology,[32] the peculiar nature — again from the standpoint of more "classical" revolutionary ideologies — of their response to economic encroachment by the Mexican state and the threat posed by NAFTA.[33] Actually, quite a lot of cultural analysis having to do with the decentralization of Mayan governmental and social forms and the like would also be required to provide anything like a comprehensive overview of the Zapatistas' indigenist content.[34]

It would be a bit too facile and simplistic to merely announce that, at core, the Zapatistas are a "Mayan thing" or an "Indian thing" and to let it go at that. This is certainly true insofar as they are Mayas and, thereby, Indians. But at another level still, and I think more importantly, they are conscious indigenists. This is the ingredient which not only completes the particular portion of their philosophical makeup I've been trying to reveal, but which makes them truly a force to be reckoned with, not only in Mexico, or Central America, or Latin America, or the Americas as a whole, but globally.

The significance of the point here was perhaps best explained by Bernard Neitschmann, a cultural geographer at the University of California at Berkeley, in an article published in *Cultural Survival Quarterly* in 1988.[35] Neitschmann did a survey of every armed conflict worthy of the name he could identify on the planet at the time, and he came up with some rather startling results: of the 125 or so "hot wars" he cataloged, fully 85 percent were being waged by specific indigenous peoples, or amalgamations of indigenous peoples, against one or more nation-states — capitalist, socialist, and "nonaligned" alike — which claimed traditional native territories as their own. In each case, despite the vast range of cultural differentiation evident among the various indigenous peoples involved around the world, the crux of their agendas was precisely the same: the insurgents had taken up arms, usually against vastly superior forces, to assert their rights to sovereignty and self-determination within their own defined (or definable) homelands.[36]

It is vital to understand that in expressly identifying themselves as an indigenist movement, the Zapatistas have elected to link themselves not only with their own Mayan tradition of resistance, or the American Indian tradition of resistance more generally, but with the resistance of all indigenous peoples everywhere to nation-state colonization, exploitation, and domination. Hence, the outbreak of armed struggle in Chiapas — and the incipiently comparable situations emerging in its wake in the Mexican provinces of Oaxaca and Guerrero[37] — should be read in terms of the protracted armed struggles waged by the Karins against the governments of Burma and India, the Euskadi (Basques) against Spain, the Tamils against Sri Lanka, the Irish against Great Britain, the Polisario Front against Morocco, the West Papuans against New Guinea, and so on.[38] Indeed, as two of Castañeda's colleagues, also ex-guerrilleros, have noted, the situation in Chiapas already reflects this pattern: "The war is going to be much longer than one can imagine, it is going to be a war of attrition."[39]

So pervasive is this kind of conflict at the present historical juncture that, when he aggregated it, Neitschmann concluded that it constituted a "Third World War."[40] From there, he went on to predict that, although the implications of the phenomenon had yet to be widely apprehended, much less appreciated, armed struggle by indigenous nations against subordination to nation-states would likely redefine the geopolitical landscape during the next generation. This was especially true, he felt, given the collapse of the Western "socialist alternative" to capitalist or post-capitalist domination of the world. In "real world" terms, this is the essence of indigenism. And the Zapatista revolt is most definitely an important — I would say *critical* — part of it.

> Militant Indian struggles have already proven to be crucial in radical insurgencies throughout the hemisphere, including just across the border from Chiapas in Guatemala. The thought that these indigenous struggles might become the cutting edge of multi-ethnic resistance by the victims of neoliberalism must send chills down the backs of strategic planners in Washington and Mexico City [and many other places as well].[41]

A dozen years ago, at the onset of the major conflict between the Sandinista government of Nicaragua and the Sumu, Rama, and Miskito peoples of the country's Atlantic Coast region, some of us analyzed the situation as being one in which the Left demonstrated basically the same contempt for indigenous rights as the Right.[42] What we said at the time was that unless the Sandinistas fundamentally altered their posture vis-à-vis the national rights of the Sumus, Ramas, and Miskitos, they would not ultimately be preferable to the Right so far as the Indians were concerned. And, since it was plain that the Sandinistas needed the support of the Indians to survive, a failure to alter their posture in that respect would mean that their revolution would fail. Well, the fact is that the government in Managua never did reach an accommodation with the Indians, and the revolution failed.[43]

By that point, having taken a hard look at the demographic realities of Latin America, and the ideological tenets the Left was advancing as a basis for revolution in those localities, we had already concluded that the attitudes displayed by the Sandinistas were endemic. What we said in response was that there aren't going to be any more revolutions in this hemisphere until the Left addresses what it calls the National Question with reference to indigenous peoples, and in a manner which is satisfactory to those peoples themselves.[44] The Left has not done this — has in fact refused to acknowledge any real need to do it — with the result that there has been a dramatic ebbing of revolutionary potential in this hemisphere since 1980.

It's true that we could get into some kind of elaborate discussion of the effects of the Soviet dissolution on Left revolutionary potential in the Americas, but I want to head that one off right now. First, whatever you may have thought of it, the USSR is gone, and any revolutionary potential it may ever have generated in this hemisphere went along with it. Second, a major reason for its demise was the way *it* — just like the Sandinistas — suppressed the self-determining aspirations of its "minority nationalities." So, the seeds of self-destruction of these sorts of Leninist states — and I want to lump China and Vietnam into this categorization — were contained all along within the supposedly revolutionary ideologies upon which they were founded.[45] The wisdom of trying to revive something of that sort as a revolutionary motivator, or as a working model for social transformation, utterly escapes me.

Left revolution, here and elsewhere, is currently no more than a dead horse. It foundered on its own "internal contradictions," so to speak. There's no percentage in beating it any more. What's needed at this point is a whole new horse. Now, let me turn back to Santamaría Gómez, himself a leftist of the newMarxian persuasion, and in my judgment somewhat bewildered as a result by the whole set of circumstances pertaining in Chiapas:

> At a time when the wave of revolutions in Central America has been receding, when few have believed in revolution at all, the Zapatistas have gone ahead and started one . . . It is remarkable what a powerful impact the EZLN has had, seemingly against all odds. They have done it by defying the conventional wisdom, and they have apparently done it on their own . . . They have found widespread sympathy in Mexico and abroad — not for the war, necessarily, but for the justice of their cause, and for their passionate demand to break with five hundred years of oppression.[46]

In other words, the Zapatistas — and the *indigenismo* they incarnate — represent the revitalization of revolutionary potential in America. Given that they are part of a global struggle premised in the same indigenist principles they manifest, they can be said equally to represent the revitalization of world revolutionary potential. At each level, they make this representation in ways which are not so much distinct from but antithetical to not just the prevailing capitalist order, but the standard "oppositional" dogmas of Marxism-Leninism-Maoism as well. They do so in ways which are corrective to the modes of oppression intrinsic to both capitalism and its Western alternatives: ways which finally and truly *do* lead toward self-determination for all peoples, no matter how small or "primitive"; ways which really *do* point toward the dissolution of colonial structures, both external and internal; directions which, if pursued to their logical terminus, would actually culminate in the dismantling of the crushing weight of statism which the past several centuries of eurosupremacism have imposed upon us all.

To conclude, the characteristics of Zapatismo I've covered, in however hopscotched and cursory a fashion, are things to be applauded, to be supported, to be replicated whenever and wherever possible. In them I see a solid basis for getting beyond the theoretical/practical impasse in which we presently find ourselves, for eventually discovering a bona fide route to liberation. It was, I suspect, from a similar frame of mind that Che Guevara once called for "two, three, many Vietnams." For my part, from a very different perspective perhaps, but with absolute respect for what it was he tried to do, I would like to call for two, three, *many* Chiapas revolts.

Notes on page 246

UNDERSTANDING CHIAPAS
Peter Rosset

> We have nothing to lose, absolutely nothing, no decent roof over
> our heads, no land, no work, poor health, no food, no educa-
> tion, no right to freely and democratically choose our leaders,
> no independence from foreign interests, and no justice for our-
> selves or our children. But today we say enough is enough! We
> are the descendants of those who truly built this nation, we are
> the millions of dispossessed, and we call upon our brothers to
> join our crusade, the only option to avoid dying of starvation!
> — *EZLN Declaration of War*

WHEN THE MEXICAN STATE OF CHIAPAS WAS THRUST
upon the international scene, it called to mind recent conflicts in
neighboring Central America. But the Zapatista Army showed a
much greater degree of organization and military strength in
their first action than had the FSLN in Nicaragua, the FMLN in
El Salvador, or the URNG in Guatemala. And unlike most of the
Central American guerrilla organizations, their rank and file are
composed almost exclusively of teenagers and young adults from
the ethnic Mayan groups of the highlands.

What at second glance seems to be another ethnic conflict in
a decade of ethnic strife around the world, is both that and more.
The roots of the struggle do indeed spring from the history of
marginalization and racism to which the Maya Indians have

been subject, but their Declaration of War and other statements clearly reach out to the poor of all ethnic groups across the length and breadth of greater Mexico.

Outside of Mexico, the Zapatista uprising has at least two far-reaching implications. First, the rebellion has been widely seen as the first organized cry by the dispossessed of the New World Order. Coinciding with the implementation of NAFTA, it was a powerfully symbolic act which has been interpreted as a people's struggle against the effects of global restructuring. Never mind that the preparations for their struggle actually predate the 1980s. In the postmodern era what counts is how actions are read. Around the world, neoliberal leaders received an electrifying shock on January 1st: the social cost of their policies may express itself in ways definitely not conducive to maintaining stable investment climates. This has had a palpable effect on policymakers from Mexico to Washington, and indeed throughout the world.

Second, the Zapatista revolutionary strategy, emphasizing civil society and rejecting vanguardism, together with their initial success, is bound to influence progressive thinking everywhere. In isolated Lacandón settlements, diverse peoples developed communities based on collective decision making. In various interviews, Subcomandante Marcos has laid out a clear rejection of the vanguardism of the 1980s Mesoamerican guerrilla movements, stating in one interview that: "We do not want state power. It is civil society that must transform Mexico — we are only a small part of that civil society, the armed part — our role is to be the guarantors of the political space that civil society needs."

The civil society strategy has had enormous early success. After the EZLN retreated to their jungle hideouts, ordinary peasants were moved to seize town halls across the Chiapas highlands to demand the removal from office of corrupt local *caciques.* Time and again they said that they had been "awakened" by the Zapatistas. Other peasants in Chiapas have taken land reform into their own hands, squatting on more than 100,000 hectares of land belonging to large landowners. Marcos captivated the Mexico City middle class, and the entire Mexican political system was shaken to its very core.

Geographically, the state of Chiapas is part of Central America, the volcanic isthmus where we find the southernmost frontier of the indigenous cultures of North America. The central region is a high elevation plateau composed of steep rugged terrain, known as the Chiapas highlands. To the southwest are the fertile Pacific lowlands, to the east is the Lacandón jungle, and to the southeast lies Guatemala. Originally part of the Captaincy of Guatemala during the time of the Spanish Colony, Chiapas was annexed by Mexico following independence. Nevertheless, the highlands can be thought of culturally as the northern extension of the Altiplano of Guatemala, inhabited by closely related Mayan peoples. Today Chiapas is one of the two poorest states of Mexico.

The historical roots of today's conflict go back to the preconquest era when the Pacific lowland areas served as the breadbasket of the indigenous civilizations. With the arrival of the Spanish, however, indigenous peoples were progressively pushed off those lands by the expansion of plantations owned by Spanish-speaking *ladinos*. By the turn of the century the fertile lands of the region were mostly occupied by cattle ranchers and sugar, coffee, and cotton plantations, while the indigenous people of Chiapas were forced to farm the thin, rocky soils found on the steep slopes of the highlands. Not only did the original inhabitants of the region lose their lands, but they have also been subject to centuries of fierce racism and discrimination on the part of the dominant *ladino* society, which continues virtually unabated to this day. Yet the last forty years have probably contributed as much to the current situation as did the six hundred years since the Conquest.

In the 1950s the shrinking plots of land in the highlands could no longer support the Indian population and the poorest began to migrate toward the last frontier, the sparsely populated Lacandón jungle area to the east. There these colonists cleared tracts of rain forest land and exposed red clay soils that lose their fertility within one to three crop cycles. They were soon joined by Spanish-speaking peasants fleeing poverty in many other areas of Mexico, many of them with experiences in local peasant revolts.

Meanwhile those who remained behind in the Chiapas highlands saw a dramatic redrawing of social configurations within the indigenous villages during the 1970s and 1980s. In the late seventies the oil boom in bordering states initiated a cycle of social polarization in the highlands that was accelerated by the debt crisis of the early eighties. Class lines were accentuated within the communities, with the increasing alignment of local, indigenous elites, or *caciques* with the governing party, and the emergence of a burgeoning underclass of the newly dispossessed. These latter families once again initiated a cycle of migration and colonization of still unexploited lands in nearby lower elevation areas.

Together with the indigenous peoples of the neighboring state of Oaxaca, the lowland colonists and the destitute in the highlands were the poorest, most desperate people in Mexico. As if that were not already enough, the conditions faced by most of them have worsened substantially during the past ten years, as successive Mexican presidents have implemented structural adjustment and free trade policies that have eroded fully 40 percent of the purchasing power of the Mexican poor. Finally, Mexican president Carlos Salinas's controversial Solidarity antipoverty program never reached the Lacandón area to any significant extent. Thus it should come as no surprise that the lower elevation Lacandón settlements of highland colonists should be the incubators for armed rebellion.

What lessons should we be taking from the events in Chiapas? One answer is that you can't force a people to live under progressively more intolerable conditions for centuries and not expect a violent response. Beyond that, we can use these events to better understand the dynamics of rural indigenous communities.

Conventional wisdom among anthropologists and others has long assumed that such communities are relatively insular units, with little relationship or integration into the larger, nonindigenous or nonpeasant society. According to such reasoning they engage primarily in farming activities, and only relate to the nation-state through a defensive or reactive posture. If we believe this we are forced into a sort of black-and-white form of thinking: either we romanticize their lifestyle, imagining it to be pristine, unaffected by and better than modern life, or we assume that they are backward and inefficient, an obstacle to modernization. These polarized viewpoints have cut across the political spectrum, with indigenous rights activists and many traditional conservatives tending toward the first view, and socialist state planners and neoliberals agreeing upon the latter.

None of these positions have been translated into effective policy, however — witness rural development debacles across the world — and it is clear that we are now in desperate need of a more nuanced understanding of peasant societies.

A recently completed study of highland Chiapas by Stanford University anthropologist George Collier is a good first step toward such an understanding. By focusing on the oil boom and the subsequent debt crisis he has found a much more subtle and far reaching degree of connectedness than previously thought between apparently "insular" Mayan communities and the national economy of Mexico.

The boom in the nearby oil fields and the employment that was generated in related construction, transport, and development activities exerted a pull that drew able-bodied men out of the highlands and into remunerated wage labor, in some cases quite well remunerated, for periods of up to several years. This labor exodus led to a collapse of highland agriculture. Conventional views of peasant societies would have predicted that once this process had occurred it would be irreversible — that peasant agriculture would never recover. Yet Collier found that when employment opportunities in the lowlands evaporated during Mexico's 1982 debt crisis, Mayans returned en masse to the highlands and in fact revitalized their farming activities. This revitalized peasant agriculture was, however, very different from the traditional agriculture that existed before the oil boom. Farmers had not previously used chemical fertilizers and pesticides, instead growing corn with shifting cultivation in which the lengthy fallow period allowed the notoriously poor soils to recover some degree of fertility before being planted again. The key productive input was labor, for clearing and preparation of fields but especially for weeding during the growing season.

When the men returned to their villages after the oil boom they brought with them two things, the money some of them had saved and a taste for modern technology. They capitalized their agricultural production via the introduction of fertilizers and herbicides, which are now ubiquitous in the highlands. This change in agricultural practices has contributed to two profound transformations, changing both the highland landscape and social relations within indigenous communities.

Aerial photographs show quite dramatically the change in the landscape surrounding Apas, a highland community for which Collier has assembled three decades of data. The area in crops dropped substantially during the oil boom, but later rebounded to cover an area much greater than ever before — a consequence of the decline of shifting cultivation. Fertilizers are now used to provide soil fertility in place of the fallow cycle, and herbicides allow continuous use of land that would once have been left fallow for several years. From a landscape that was dominated by second growth and forest it has been transformed to one dominated by annual crops.

This has had an important environmental consequence: a dramatic increase in soil erosion as the heavy rains wash away the earth that is barely protected by annual crops. This degradation of the land and associated loss of soil fertility lowers the ability of the land to sustain human populations, contributing to the tendency toward outward migration.

While land and family labor were once the essential production factors used in highland farming, the capital to purchase chemicals and to hire additional labor has now become the most important "input." The newly competitive, commercial nature of agriculture has meant that access to capital has become the axis around which farming activities have been reorganized. Those who accumulated more capital during the oil boom, particularly those who invested in trucks and other transport vehicles, now control highland agriculture through money lending, sharecropping, land rental, labor contracting, transport, and other activities. These are the *caciques*. People at the other extreme have become the newly destitute referred to above, in some cases working as day laborers but in many cases emigrating from their communities, sometimes voluntarily and sometimes forcibly, as political, religious, and community relations have fractured along the lines of the economic polarization wrought in agriculture. These people have founded new communities in the interstices between the older ones, or have migrated permanently, in some cases to urban areas and in other cases to the agricultural frontier in the Lacandón lowlands, where they have joined the earlier colonists.

The earlier colonists were perhaps in even worse shape than the more recent arrivals, as the isolated nature of the area in which they live meant that few, if any, of them participated in the oil boom employment, and because their soils are even worse than those of the highlands. It is this area of frontier settlements in jungle clearings that has produced the Zapatistas. This is where the poorest people in Mexico live, and while most of them speak indigenous languages of highland origin, the presence of Spanish-speaking migrants from elsewhere may have provided the final ingredient of insurgent peasant ideology. Worsening economic conditions of recent years and developments such as NAFTA, with its provisions for lowering the price of the corn they produce, seem to have triggered events leading to the armed struggle that these poorest of the poor have now carried to the highlands from whence many of them came.

One factor that the Zapatistas have referred to repeatedly in their communiqués is the reform of Article 27 of the Mexican Constitution that President Salinas pushed through in preparation for NAFTA. This amendment ended the agrarian reform that has been carried out sporadically since the Mexican Revolution, thus effectively dashing the hopes of landless peasants of ever owning their own small farms.

The nuances revealed by Collier's work explain two things in the news that at first seemed contradictory. First, why has there been a mixed reaction to the uprising in highland communities? Why were rebel prisoners beaten by townspeople in Ocosingo, while other local civilians expressed support for the guerrilla? This ceases to be a paradox once we grasp the nonhomogeneity of these villages. Although all seem poor to the outside observer, there are in fact townspeople who are wealthy by local standards, who have hitched their fate to the dominant political party, and who thus have much to lose in an uprising which surely is at least in part against *them*.

The second apparent contradiction is found in the rhetoric used by the Zapatistas in their pronouncements. If this is an ethnic rebellion, and indeed the vast majority of the fighters barely speak Spanish, why do their press releases contain no statements of ethnic nationalism? Rather than rejecting the legitimacy of the *ladino* Mexican state, they use the Constitution to justify their actions. Their "Declaration of the Lacandón Jungle" contains the following language, reminiscent of the U.S. Declaration of Independence:

> We call upon Article 39 of the Mexican Constitution which states "the people have at all times the inalienable right to alter or change the nature of their government." Therefore, in accordance with our Constitution, we issue this DECLARATION OF WAR . . . People of Mexico, we call for your total participation in this struggle for work, land, housing, food, health care, education independence, liberty, democracy, justice and peace.

This is no declaration of ethnic warfare. It is strikingly different from the words used by the Shining Path in Peru or the Bosnian Serbs. In fact, taken as a whole, the various press releases of the Zapatistas paint a picture of an uprising of the poor, regardless of ethnicity, calling for basic human rights. It is likely that the mixing in of Spanish speaking peasants in the Lacandón settlements contributed to the inclusionary, rather than exclusionary, nature of their rhetoric.

The broad appeal of the Zapatista message led to a degree of David vs. Goliath sympathy among the general population of Mexico, provoking large solidarity marches. And it thrust the very nature of the neoliberal economic model of the Salinas administration onto the national agenda for discussion, as urban elites woke up to the reality that there are now two Mexicos: the yuppie Mexico in the capital and northern cities that has fed upon market liberalization and NAFTA-related investment, and the ever larger and ever more marginalized poor Mexico. The easy transition that President Salinas expected for his hand-picked successor suddenly was not so easy. Concessions were made on electoral reform that were unthinkable even last year, and topics that were taboo, such as the role of the military in Mexican society, are now openly debated. It would appear that the Zapatistas have let the genie of popular inconformity out of the bottle, and it remains to be seen if Salinas and the PRI will be able to get it back in.

What sort of changes would be necessary to provide a decent life to the indigenous people of Chiapas and poor peasants throughout Mexico? Is peasant farming an anachronism that must disappear if we are to eliminate rural poverty?

These questions are linked, and in answering with a qualified no to the second, we can approach a response to the first. As social relations and land tenure are currently configured in Chiapas, and indeed across Mexico, peasant agriculture is not viable. But that is not an intrinsic characteristic, but rather the product of trade policies and land concentration.

What is needed is both a new land distribution program and a favorable macroeconomic environment. Mayan communities must be given communal *ejido* holdings in fertile lowland areas, with guarantees of secure tenure. This is not so far-fetched as it seems, as previous Mexican land reforms have given some villages limited access to quality lowland farmland which they work on a seasonal basis. Fair credit must be made available and crop prices should be supported sufficiently to allow for a sustainable livelihood, much as is done in Japan, Taiwan, and elsewhere. This is best achieved through barriers to cheap imports rather than subsidies, thereby avoiding deficit spending. Finally corrupt local authorities linked to the PRI must be thrown out, as has been demanded in the many peasant takeovers of towns that have taken place since the start of the Zapatista uprising.

Of course these changes would require democratization, some rollback of NAFTA and the restoration of Article 27 of the

Constitution, but these are just the sort of issues that the Zapatistas have thrust into the national debate in Mexico.

What will the future bring? Will the rebellion in Chiapas serve as an effective warning against the excesses of structural adjustment? And does the novel ideology of the EZLN mark a shift away from the recent trend towards ethnic nationalism among armed movements? Does the Zapatista rebellion mean that recent announcements of the death of the armed Left in Latin America have been premature and that indeed, we may see more uprisings against the wasteland that free market ideology has created in the global south?

What we can be sure of is that the Zapatistas have managed to awaken the world's progressive forces from the lethargy and depression brought on by the collapse of the socialist bloc and the apparent triumph of neoliberalism and free trade ideology. And for that we can be thankful.

UP FROM THE BOTTOM
Iain A. Boal

> If the rebellions of the southeast lose, as they lose in the north, the center, and east, it is not because they lack number and support, it is because wind is the fruit of the earth, and it has its own season, and matures not in books filled with regrets.
> — *EZLN Communiqué*

IN THE FIRST WEEK OF THIS YEAR, AS NEWS OF THE uprising in Chiapas began to blow north, old friends and students of E. P. Thompson were gathering in San Francisco to commemorate the life and work of the English radical who pioneered "history from below." He had thundered against a triumphalist history of the Industrial Revolution; he devoted himself to "the blind alleys, the lost causes, and the losers," seeking to rescue them, in his famous phrase, "from the enormous condescension of posterity." This retrieval was for him a morally necessary act, but by no means a sentimental one, since "the greater part of the world today is still undergoing problems of industrialization, and of the formation of democratic institutions, analogous in many ways to our own experience during the

Industrial Revolution. Causes which were lost in England might, in Asia or Africa, yet be won." Or, he might have said, the Americas.

This tentative optimism gave way, thirty years later, to a bleaker view. The relentless global penetration of a brutal capitalism was no longer meeting resistance in the old utopian terms. The collective imaginary had, it seemed, been stuffed with the cornucopia of industrial goods. He remarked on "the readiness of the human species to define its needs and satisfactions in material market terms — and to throw all the globe's resources onto the market . . . The engineer of this catastrophe will be economic man." At the end of his life, he was bracing us for bad weather. He saw his writings as a message in a bottle, flung into the typhoon. "We shall not ever return to precapitalist human nature, yet a reminder of its alternative needs, expectations and codes may renew our sense of nature's range of possibilities."

The militant core of resistance to the immiseration visited upon the world's first modern industrial state were the Luddites, those English weavers of the early nineteenth century who smashed the mechanical looms that were throwing them out of work and into starvation. Given the stereotype of the Luddite as a mindless, antitechnology, backward-looking wrecker, it is impossible to grasp the actual dynamic of resistance and accommodation. Why was it that the Luddites sometimes broke old frames while leaving new machinery intact? It all depended on the social relations of production and the conditions under which the power looms were to be used. In the case of Chiapas, amid certain peasant resistance to technological innovation, there is a predictable contradiction between "traditional" highland agriculturalists and post–oil boom farmers using capital-intensive equipment and petrochemical fertilizers. These kinds of innovation can create deep fissures in the community, sometimes with shattering effects on the moral economy, as, for example, the introduction of the snowmobile had among the pastoralists of Lapland. This is not to say that the sanction of "tradition" expresses anything timeless, but rather a historic balance of social forces.

From a relatively comfortable position in "the North" it would be grotesque to cheer on the restoration of a peasantry. To do so would be to argue for the preservation of exploitation, and the leading of lives in which the burden of physical work is often devastating and oppressive. John Berger is right: in a just world such a class would no longer exist. Yet the *way* in which, in the great arc of the last half millennium, the world's peasantry is entering into extinction is exemplary of the catastrophe of enclosure.

It was Thomas Moore, in *Utopia*, who first savagely portrayed the devouring of people and land by sheep at the onset of agrarian capitalism in Europe. Karl Polanyi called the enclosures a revolution of the rich against the poor that decimated the population, turned the soil into dust, and the peasants into beggars.

The Luddite movement and the Chiapas insurrection are both moments and modes of resistance in what Polanyi called "the great transformation" to the global market. This vast historical and worldwide process is, in its drive for the essential commodification of land and labor, one of enclosure. It has many forms: the privatizing of communal land ("commons," "*ejidos*"), the incarceration of production into what are called "factories," the corralling of the landless dispossessed into ghettos, barracks, prisons, asylums, schools. What polite scholarship calls "urbanization" — and Mexico City is its epitome — is itself a result of the seizing of livelihood from the rural poor. In response, the poor take back the means of living; the ruling class calls it "crime."

The regnant narrative, whose keywords are "progress" and "modernity"and "development," conjures its extinct dinosaurs, such as the Luddites, and its living coelocanths, that is, the residual peasantry and a handful of quaint enclaves, "tribes" who constitute our contemporary ancestors. That is the metaphysic of modernity, whether in its classical capitalist form or in the form, until recently, of its rebellious Marxist sibling.

This myth of modernity is rubbish. There is nothing unmodern or archaic about the deserted ruins of Ireland, about the "ethnic" killing fields of Rwanda, about the eroded hillsides of Chiapas — any more than slavery is prior to and incompatible with capitalism. There is nothing "backward" about barrios and *favelas* without water or electricity. The pictures from Haiti truly reveal one of modernity's faces, as did the footage from south central Los Angeles.

One of the most vital tasks in the recovery of the casualties of this bloody business is the contesting of the ideology of progress based on an evolutionary model of societal development that condemns them and those like them inescapably to the past. By this cool logic the Luddites and the Chiapanecos are cast together, across time and space, into the lumber room of history. And others along with them — bandits, pirates, primitive rebels, Captain Swing, the French peasants of 1851, the artisan anarchists that Marxists (until recently) felt entitled to sneer at.

The illiterate communiqués of the Luddites, which threatened the mill owners with collective bargaining by riot (and always signed "General Ludd") did nothing to dispel class contempt or the notion that the anonymous machine-breakers were tongue-tied artisans beached by the storm of progress. Tony Harrison's poem "On not being Milton" bitterly celebrates their broken language — the "lumpen mass of Ludding morphemes."

At the memorial gathering for E. P. Thompson we spoke of our reaction to events in Chiapas. What to make of the communiqués signed "Subcomandante Marcos?" These texts are, to say the least, unusual material for "history from below," where the annalist of the illiterate, the silent and the silenced is typically forced to use sources that lie, as Thompson put it, like "lobster traps, on the sea-bottom ... catching many curious literary creatures which never, in normal circumstances, break the bland surface of the waters" of traditional historiography.

Was it appropriate to listen for the authentic Mayan voice beneath the colonial Spanish gloss? Leslie Lopez, of the Watsonville Human Rights Committee, while working on the translation of the Zapatista texts, realized that Marcos "was a translator as well. He too was trying to translate several indigenous languages and get it right. It was an exhilarating moment." For some, Marcos's communiqués placed the Zapatista press office in a postmodern bunker in the mountains — no stammering scrawl of the Luddites there, but a vivid pastiche of proverbial wisdom, military and diplomatic protocols, and metropolitan argot.

We must abandon talk of "authenticity," without losing the distinction between such a tactical pastiche and a "mere" simulacral politics, always already captured by the machine of mediation. Actually, the contemporary conditions of the globalized and integrated spectacle should insistently prompt questions about the relation between movements of resistance, their representations and their reception — in this case, a vernacular insurgency that has figured itself, not in indigenous terms, but as the continuation of a national revolution, then filtered to us through the Mexican and international press.

In these etherialized circuits of communication, let some news blow back south. There is no substance to the dreams of *homo economicus*, fantasies of salvation at the hands of the technicians of either consumption or production. The longing for a better world will need to arise at the imagined meeting place of many movements of resistance, as many as there are sites of closure and exclusion. The resistance will be as transnational as capital. Because enclosure takes myriad forms, so shall resistance to it. The dispersed movements therefore need to see the common ground in, say, the fight *against* the final eradication of the redwoods in North America and *for* an extractive indigenous economy in Amazonia.

Here, then, is the other legacy willed by Edward Thompson to those who come after. A second message in the bottle, as it were, besides the priceless recording of the active resistance on behalf of a moral economy and a customary consciousness. To speak of Luddism, is to take only the most scorned and discredited of the thousand figures our culture provides us of hopelessness and backwardness and "futile" resistance. The restoration of the Luddites, accordingly, invites the widest generalizing, to enable a strategic — even a mythic — connection, via the central idea of "enclosure," between the lost struggles of the handloom weavers against factory discipline and starvation, and contemporary forms of resistance to the megamachine — against the automobilism and zoning that denatures city life, against the mechanization of birth, against racist surveillance and the criminalization of poverty, against the iron cage of bureaucracy, against state borders and identities, and by the peoples of Chiapas against the storm from above.

TIME BOMBS
Noam Chomsky

MAJOR CHANGES IN THE GLOBAL ORDER OVER THE past quarter-century have led to a huge increase in unregulated financial capital and a radical shift in its use, from long-term investment and trade to speculation.

The effect has been to undermine national economic planning as governments are compelled to preserve market "credibility," driving economies toward what Cambridge University economist John Eatwell calls "a low-growth, high-unemployment equilibrium," with declining real wages, increasing poverty and inequality for the many, and profits for the few.

The parallel process of internationalization of production provides multinational corporations with new weapons to undermine working people in the West. Workers must now accept an end to their "luxurious" lifestyles and agree to "flexibility of labor markets" (i.e., not knowing whether you have a job tomorrow). The return of most of Eastern Europe to its Third World origins enhances these prospects considerably. The attack on worker rights, social standards, and functioning democracy throughout the world reflects this new economic order. So does the current recovery in the United States — the first one in which wages are declining for most of the work force, inequality is increasing, unemployment is scarcely changing, and more than a quarter of new jobs are provided by temporary help agencies (one of which is now the nation's largest private employer, *Fortune* magazine reports).

The triumphalism among narrow elite sectors is quite understandable, as is the mounting despair and anger outside privileged circles.

The New Year's Day uprising of Indian peasants in Chiapas can be understood in this general context. The uprising coincided with the enactment of the North American Free Trade Agreement (NAFTA). The Zapatista army called NAFTA a "death sentence" for Indians, a gift to the rich that will deepen the divide between narrowly concentrated wealth and mass misery, destroying what remains of their indigenous society.

The NAFTA connection is partly symbolic; the problems are far deeper. "We are the product of 500 years of struggle," the Zapatista Declaration of War states. The struggle today is "for work, land, housing, food, health care, education, independence, freedom, democracy, justice and peace."

The Indian peasants are the most aggrieved victims of government policies. But their distress is widely shared. "Anyone who has the opportunity to be in contact with the millions of Mexicans who live in extreme poverty knows that we are living with a time bomb," Mexican columnist Pilar Valdes observes.

In the past decade of economic reform, the number of people

living in extreme poverty in rural areas of Mexico has increased by almost a third. Half of the country's total population lacks resources to meet basic needs, a dramatic increase since 1980. Following World Bank–International Monetary Fund (IMF) prescriptions, agricultural production was shifted to export and animal feeds — a policy that benefited agribusiness, foreign consumers, and affluent sectors in Mexico at the expense of the general population. Malnutrition became a major health problem, agricultural employment declined, productive lands were abandoned, and Mexico began to import massive amounts of food. Real wages in manufacturing fell sharply. Labor's share in the gross domestic product, which had risen until the mid-seventies, has since declined by well over a third.

These are standard concomitants of neoliberal reforms. IMF studies show "a strong and consistent pattern of reduction of labor's share of income" under the impact of its "stabilization programs" in Latin America, economist Manuel Pastor observes.

The Mexican secretary of commerce hailed the fall in wages as an inducement to foreign investors. So it is, along with Mexico's repression of labor, lax enforcement of environmental regulations, and the general orientation of social policy to the desires of the privileged minority. Such policies are naturally welcomed by the manufacturing and financial institutions that are extending their control over the global economy with the assistance of mislabeled "free trade" agreements.

NAFTA is expected to drive large numbers of workers off the land, contributing to rural misery and a surplus of labor. Manufacturing employment, which declined under the reforms, is expected to fall more sharply. A study by Mexico's leading business journal, *El Financiero*, predicted that Mexico would lose almost a quarter of its manufacturing industry and 14 percent of its jobs in the first two years after the enactment of

NAFTA. "Economists predict that several million Mexicans will probably lose their jobs in the first five years after the accord takes effect," Tim Golden reported in the *New York Times*. These processes should depress wages still further while increasing profits and social polarization, with predictable effects in the United States and Canada.

A large part of the appeal of NAFTA, as its advocates have regularly stressed, is that it "locks in" neoliberal reforms. These reforms have reversed years of progress in labor rights and economic development, bringing mass impoverishment and suffering along with enrichment for the few and for foreign investors. To Mexico's economy generally, this "economic virtue" has brought "little reward," the London *Financial Times* observes. Mexico's "eight years of textbook market economic policies," the *Times* notes, produced only slight growth, most of it attributable to unparalleled financial assistance from the World Bank and the United States. High interest rates have partially reversed the capital flight that was a major factor in Mexico's debt crisis, but debt service is nevertheless a growing burden, its largest component now being the internal debt owed to the Mexican rich.

Not surprisingly, there was substantial opposition to the plan to "lock in" this model of development. Historian Seth Fein, writing from Mexico City, described large demonstrations against NAFTA as "well articulated, if too-little-noticed in the United States, cries of frustration against government policies — involving repeal of labor, agrarian and education rights stipulated in the nation's popularly revered 1917 Constitution — that appear to many Mexicans as the real meaning of NAFTA and U.S. foreign policy here."

A November 1, 1993, "Communication of Mexican Bishops on NAFTA" condemned the agreement, along with the economic policies of which it is a part, because of their deleterious social effects. They reiterated the concern of the 1992

Conference of Latin American Bishops that "the market economy . . . not become something absolute to which everything is sacrificed, accentuating the inequality and the marginalization of a large portion of the population."

The agreement was also opposed by many workers, including those in the largest nongovernmental union. In the *Los Angeles Times*, Juanita Darling described the great anxiety that Mexican workers feel about the erosion of their "hard-won labor rights," which are likely to "be sacrificed as companies, trying to compete with foreign companies, look for ways to cut costs." Unionists and other critics warned of NAFTA's impact on wages, workers' rights, and the environment, the loss of sovereignty, the increased protection for corporate and investor rights, and the undermining of options for sustainable growth.

It has not taken long for such fears to be realized. Shortly after the NAFTA vote in Congress, workers were fired from Mexican Honeywell and GE plants for attempting to organize independent unions. This is standard practice. The Ford Motor Co. fired its entire Mexican work force at one plant in 1987, eliminating the union contract and rehiring workers at far lower salaries. Brutal repression crushed protests. Volkswagen, with the backing of the Institutional Revolutionary Party (PRI), followed suit in 1992, firing its fourteen thousand Mexican workers and rehiring only those who renounced independent union leaders. These are central components on the "economic miracle" that is to be "locked in" by NAFTA.

A few days after the NAFTA vote, the U.S. Senate passed what Senator Orrin Hatch (R-Utah) called "the finest anti-crime package in history." The legislation calls for 100,000 new police, high-security regional prisons, boot camps for young offenders, extension of the death penalty, and harsher sentencing, as well as other onerous measures. But even law enforcement experts interviewed by the press doubted that the legislation would have much effect on crime, because it did not deal with the causes of social disintegration that produce violent criminals. Primary among these are the social and economic realities polarizing American society, which have been carried another step forward by NAFTA. The concept of "efficiency," as defined by those of wealth and privilege, offers nothing to the growing sectors of the population that are useless for profit-making, and thus have been driven to poverty and despair. If they cannot be confined to urban slums, they will have to be controlled in some other way.

Like the timing of the Zapatista rebellion, the legislative coincidence was of more than mere symbolic significance.

The NAFTA debate focused largely on job flows, about which little is known. But we can more confidently predict that wages will fall rather broadly. "Many economists think NAFTA could drag down pay, because lower Mexican wages could have a gravitational effect on the wages of Americans," Steven Pearlstein reported in the *Washington Post*. That is expected even by NAFTA advocates, who recognize that less-skilled workers — about 70 percent of the work force — are likely to suffer wage loss.

A *New York Times* review of the expected effects of NAFTA in the New York region reached similar conclusions. Gainers would be "the region's banking, telecommunications and service firms," including insurance companies, investment houses, corporate law firms, the PR industry, management consultants, and the like. Some manufacturers, primarily in high-tech industry, publishing, and pharmaceuticals may also gain as a result of increased protection for intellectual property-protection designed to ensure that major corporations control the technology of the future. But there will also be losers, "predominantly women, blacks and Hispanics," and "semi-skilled production workers" generally; that is, most of the population in New York City, where 40 percent of the children already live below the poverty line, suffering health and educational disabilities that "lock them in" to a bitter fate.

Noting that real wages for production and nonsupervisory workers have fallen to the level of the sixties, the congressional Office of Technology Assessment (OTA), in an analysis of the executive version of NAFTA, predicted that unless significantly modified it "could further lock the United States into a low-wage, low-productivity future." Revisions proposed by the OTA, labor, and other critics were mostly ignored.

The version of NAFTA that was enacted is likely to accelerate what the *Wall Street Journal* called a "welcome development of transcendent importance": the reduction of U.S. labor costs to below the levels of all major industrial countries apart from England. (Until 1985, hourly pay for American workers had been higher than the other G-7 countries.) In a globalized economy, the impact is worldwide, as competitors must accommodate. GM can move to Mexico, or now to Poland, where it can find workers at a fraction of the cost of Western labor and be protected by a 30 percent tariff. Volkswagen can move to the Czech Republic to benefit from similar protection, taking the profits and leaving the government with the costs. Daimler-Benz can make similar arrangements in Alabama. Capital can move freely, and workers and communities suffer the consequences. Meanwhile, the huge growth of unregulated speculative capital imposes powerful pressures against stimulative government policies.

There are many factors driving global society toward a low-wage, low-growth, high-profit future, with increasing polarization and social disintegration. Another consequence is the fading of meaningful and democratic processes as decision making is vested in private institutions and the quasi-governmental structures that are coalescing around them, what the *Financial Times* calls a "de facto world government" that operates in secret and without accountability.

These developments have little to do with economic liberalism, a concept of diminishing significance in a world in which a vast component of "trade" consists of centrally managed intrafirm transactions (which constitute half of all U.S. exports to Mexico, for example — "exports" that never enter the Mexican market). Meanwhile, private power demands and receives protection from market forces, as in the past. It was quite appropriate for President Clinton, at the Seattle Asia-Pacific summit, to offer as his model for the "free market" future the Boeing Corp., which would not be the country's leading exporter, nor probably even exist, were it not for the huge public subsidy from the Pentagon it has always received.

The protest of Indian peasants in Chiapas gives only a bare glimpse of time bombs waiting to explode, not only in Mexico.

NATIVE INTELLIGENCE: NAFTA IS UNCONSTITUTIONAL

Jack D. Forbes

PRESIDENT CLINTON CLAIMED A VICTORY WHEN the North American Free Trade Agreement was passed by Congress, but in reality he lost. NAFTA was passed illegally as an ordinary act of legislation, when it is, in fact, a *treaty*. A treaty is defined as an agreement or contract between sovereign states, and international "agreements" that require the approval of Congress are certainly treaties. The U.S. Constitution absolutely requires that any treaty must obtain a two-thirds affirmative vote in the Senate (see Article II, Section 2 of the Constitution), which means that NAFTA would have to have won with 68 votes, but it received only 61. So NAFTA is not law, despite President Clinton's signature.

The Constitution of the United States establishes a federal system of government, which means that most powers are distributed between the central (federal) government in Washington, D.C., and the various state and tribal governments elsewhere. Tribes have equal powers with the states, since the Interstate Commerce Clause gives the federal government the right "to regulate commerce with foreign nations, and among the several states and with Indian tribes." NAFTA specifically includes state, provincial, and local governments but fails to recognize tribal governments or reservations. The unique legal status of indigenous tribes is ignored.

NAFTA also presents a grave danger to Native land rights, especially in Mexico. Most Native Americans in Mexico do not have specific reservations, but instead live on traditional communal lands recognized for centuries by Spanish and Mexican law, most recently by the *ejido* system. The protections of the *ejido* have now been removed by the government of President Salinas, thus making it possible for indigenous lands to be purchased by outsiders. Under NAFTA, investors from the United States with wads of dollars will be able to buy up the best lands, sources of water, and river valleys. Many Native people, unused to financial wheeling and dealing, are likely to be cheated of their ancient land rights. As a result, millions could become economic refugees in the cities, and in the United States and Canada.

It is unclear if NAFTA will pose a threat to "trust land" in the United States or Canada, but certainly all privately held Indian land will be affected. NAFTA will probably adversely affect the right of a tribe to regulate the sale of privately held lands within reservation boundaries if such regulation attempts to keep Canadian or Mexican investors out.

NAFTA also completely ignores the existence of Native groups straddling the borders, such as the Mohawks, Salish-Kootenai, Colville-Okanagan, Abenakis, Cocopas, Kamias, O'odham, Kickapoos, etc. A major agreement of this sort should have recognized Native groups split apart by the U.S.-Mexican and U.S.-Canadian borders, and included provisions for free movement, unification, and indigenous local control over governmental processes.

Legislation protecting "Indian" arts and crafts may also be wiped out, since NAFTA will prevent discrimination against Canada's and Mexico's Native craftspersons. Mexican Indians outnumber U.S. Indians at least four to one, and many are weavers, potters, and artisans. In ignoring indigenous peoples totally, the creators of NAFTA did not include a new provision protecting all Native craftspersons.

NAFTA allows Canada and Mexico and their business interests, as well as U.S. corporations, to challenge any U.S. laws, codes, or regulations adopted by any state, tribe, or local government if it is believed that such laws or regulations interfere with investing or with the sale of services or products by any Canadian or Mexican firms, or subsidiaries of U.S. firms. Thus, if a tribe has a "buy Indian" rule, that rule will be challengeable by any non-Indian entity. Similarly, any and all safety and environmental regulations will be challengeable.

Who will make the final decisions in these challenges? Not our own tribal courts, nor our state courts. A Free Trade Commission and various committees appointed by the three central governments (and very probably representing corporate interests) will make the decisions. People who were never elected to any office will have the final say. Thus, NAFTA is actually an amendment to the Constitution (as well as a treaty), since it will change our system of government by eliminating much of what is left of "states' rights" and by blocking tribal governments in their march toward sovereignty. The "federal system" will be at an end.

NAFTA represents a trend typified by the growth of the General Agreement of Trades and Tariffs (GATT) superstructure, as well as by numerous unelected regional commissions and authorities (e.g., the Los Angeles Metropolitan Transit Authority, or the New York Power Authority, or the Los Angeles Metropolitan Water District). These new "governments" are run by appointed persons and bureaucrats (technocrats) who make vital decisions but who are not democratically chosen.

Bill Clinton took an oath to uphold the U.S. Constitution, as do U.S. senators, and all are bound by its provisions. Of course, Clinton's people claim that NAFTA is simply an "agreement" and not a treaty, but that is simple semantic trickery. You can call such an agreement a "declaration," a "convention," or whatever you want, but if it is a formal agreement between sovereigns, it is always a treaty and it requires a two-thirds vote for ratification. (The genocide treaty was called the "Genocide Convention," but it required a two-thirds vote in the Senate to pass.)

We know that ex-President George Bush and his negotiators designed NAFTA as a treaty because NAFTA purports to be able to nullify the laws of the United States, of the fifty states, and of local governments if they conflict with the provisions of NAFTA. This means that NAFTA becomes a part of U.S. law, part of the "supreme law of the land." But only a treaty ratified by two-thirds vote can become part of U.S. law. A so-called non-treaty "agreement," whatever that might be, can have no legal force within the United States. The House and Senate, by simple majority vote, cannot pass a law which nullifies state and local laws and ordinances, except in certain subject areas where the Constitution grants the federal government supremacy (as in foreign affairs, defense, and the like).

Thus NAFTA as a simple law of the Senate and House cannot achieve its objectives.

The newspapers tell us that NAFTA has won. Their reporters apparently don't read the Constitution. What can we do?

Obviously some organization, state government, city, tribe, or a combination of the above must go into court to have

NAFTA declared unconstitutional, to obtain a writ against its being implemented. Organized labor should take the lead, but state, provincial, local, and tribal governments should be equally concerned about the threatened loss of the powers of self-government posed by NAFTA.

Tribes and some territories should also note that NAFTA does not appear to refer to their legal existence. Native governments as well as the territories of Guam, Samoa, and the Virgin Islands are not included in NAFTA, except under the umbrella term of "local" governments or as simply part of the "customs territory" of the United States Of course, tribal and territorial governments are not "local."

Thus it is very important that tribal and territorial governments and the Associated Free State of Puerto Rico seek to have the courts declare NAFTA to be invalid within their territories without the specific consent of their governing bodies. If this is not done, tribes take the risk of allowing themselves to be categorized simply as "local" governments, and of having their sovereign powers drastically diminished. (States, provinces, and territories also face the same loss of self-government, of course.) In addition, tribal and band governments should pass resolutions declaring that NAFTA shall be without effect within their territories, and on any lands to which they possess a claim (e.g., the Black Hills).

One objective might be to force the U.S., Canadian, and Mexican governments to agree to a renegotiation of NAFTA in which all international agreements relating to the rights of indigenous peoples, women, children, ethnic minorities, and labor can be incorporated into the treaty. Moreover, one might wish to demand that any new NAFTA be accompanied by a North American Parliament with *elected* delegates, including representation for tribes and indigenous communities. (After all, NAFTA is supposed to be patterned after the European Union, but the EU also has the European Parliament.) But of course, election means nothing unless indigenous governments, women, and ethnic minorities are guaranteed representation.

In any case, people should think about these options and not give up.

AN INDIGENOUS AMERICAN INTIFADA

by M. A. Jaimes Guerrero

THERE IS A REVOLUTION COMING FROM THE South, and indigenous peoples are in the vanguard. Grassroots revolutionaries calling themselves the Mayan Zapatistas have raised their voices in protest against NAFTA. The Chiapas rebellion is an American intifada for indigenous peoples' liberation from First World oppression and the genocidal destruction of their distinct cultures.

NAFTA's predatory strategies of international law and policy — colonization by the United States and the homogenization wrought by global corporate politics — are not new to First World power interdynamics. Since Columbian contact and conquest, the Native populations in the Americas have been under siege by extensive genocidal campaigns implemented by nationalist governments. These political agendas created the reservation system in the United States through the forced removal acts of the 1800s. This was followed by the coerced allotment that stole tribal lands, the reorganization of tribal societies in the 1930s, urban relocations in the 1940s, termination in the 1950s, an assimilation policy under the guise of "Indian self-determination," and cultural genocide that continues into the 1990s. NAFTA's historic roots can be perceived in such key Indian laws as the Trade and Intercourse Acts of 1790 to 1834 — a series of statutes that codified the Constitution's Commerce Clause, providing the federal government with the tools to enforce regulatory authority over its citizens in their intercourse with Native peoples, to the ultimate disadvantage of Native peoples with regards to their lands and cultural lifeways. The Alaska Native Claims Act of 1971 is a more contemporary manifestation of this predatory mentality: it converted the tribal nations of Alaska into thirteen regional and smaller village corporations, dissolving them as tribal entities by congressional fiat, to be incorporated into the U.S. polity — another form of termination imposed upon Native groups.

NAFTA is a vehicle for the United States' and Mexico's trilateralist ends, and as such its agenda is to obstruct Third World resistance among Native populations and to make them available to inhumane labor markets. *Covert Action News* (Winter 1993–1994) exposed the powerful network of corporate interests and their hired public relations agents, along with an elite corps from the political ranks who engineered NAFTA's passage. The notorious profit-motivated Trilateral Commission has avidly promoted the free trade deal since its inception — its membership of greedy financiers and sponsors includes former and present American presidents, as well as international corporate empire-building moguls.

Native warriors among men, women, and children, from the

very old to the very young, are rising up against the colonialist genocide, ethnocide, and ecocide that the First World powers and their political/corporate collaborators are perpetrating on them in their autochthonous homelands. Many indigenous groups and activists feel affinity and alliance with the Mayans' struggle — in the face of a long history of human rights violations — to end the exploitation of their labor and the destruction of their indigenous cultures. This is the same struggle being waged in the numerous Third World liberation fires throughout the Americas in the 1990s, from the protests of the Santiago massacre in Guatamala, to the Oka uprising in Canada, to the "gambling wars" that tribal groups are fighting for economic self-sufficiency, pitted against U.S. federal/state authorities. Even the neoconservative National Council of American Indians denounced the brutal actions of the military forces sent in by President Salinas to put down the Chiapas insurrection. Overall this Native people's movement is visionary, transforming the transitional Third World politics toward worldwide indigenous liberation.

This freedom fight is also a struggle for the land and all living beings, both human and nonhuman, and for the rights of the natural world. It is being led by the Indios, who still believe in community, culture, kinship, and an indigenous nationhood that recognizes a reciprocal relationship with the natural environment.

NAFTA has been declared "international termination" of the rights of indigenous peoples by Native delegations and organizations before the United Nations Human Rights Committee in Geneva, Switzerland. The courageous, committed revolutionaries of Chiapas are an inspiration to others to rise up against their power-mongering oppressors, and to resist the fascistic boot of the transnational corporations. They have put action into words by standing up to the oligarchs and their corporate backers for their basic human rights. They are challenging the continued genocide — both physical and cultural — perpetrated by Euroamerican imperialism in collaboration with Latin American law-and-order oppression. In the emerging New World Order that hides behind "representative democracy," NAFTA and GATT are virtual "realities" advocated by European powers and the World Trade Organization for corporate nationalism, at the expense of people, cultures, and any kind of genuine participatory peoples' democracy. To quote Marc Cooper, ". . . Chiapas is the first armed battle against the Global Market. . . ."

Hence, the tentative "peace accord," which is still being negotiated, is only a first step in countering the Eurocentrism inherent in United States–Mexican politics — a parasitic policy forced upon traditional indigenous peoples in what Chicano scholar and activist Rudolf Acuna has called "Occupied America." I hope my brothers and sisters to the South will heed the wise words proclaimed by Marie Legos, a heroic Native Californian whose cry still echos in the Native liberation movement here in the United States: "America has not shown me my terms of surrender!"

THE UNFINISHED WAR
by Juan Bañuelos

THE UPRISING OF THE INDIOS OF CHIAPAS IS A
final call for Mexico to democratize and to redress centuries of
abuse and betrayal, embodied in the lack of liberty, justice, truth,
and respect for the dignity of the ethnic peoples who inhabit the
jungles and highlands of the Southeast.

The various names that have been used for the indigenous
people who are workers — *peones, acasillados, mozos,* and
baldíos [unskilled laborers, tenant farmers, farmhands, migrant
workers] — signal their relationship to the land and to its owners, and suggest the conditions of subjugation and suffering that
the Indios have endured since the Spanish conquest. All of them
have lived in the service of a *Casa Grande* [Big House], that is,
the main building on the ranches, farms, and estates where the

"proprietary," unlawful holder of the land resides. This situation has been the cause of bloody uprisings and wars throughout the centuries. Nevertheless . . .

The Conquered Gods Are the Demons of the Conquerors

With the Zapatista uprising against the repressive system of the Mexican government, all of this has changed. In March 1994, a meeting was held in San Cristóbal de las Casas, in which representatives of different ethnic groups — Tzotziles, Tzeltales, Ch'oles, Tojolabales, Zoques — came together to analyze the uprising of their brothers and sisters. After much dialogue and deliberation, the indigenous peoples upheld the justifiable demands of the Zapatistas and declared their support for a *Nueva Vida* [New Life] and for a change in their relationship to the power structure that has dominated their lives. They decided to take the name given to the owner's house and to build a *Casa Grande* for everyone, creating a symbol of hope from what in other times had been a place and a symbol of ignominy. The *Casa Grande* thus acquired a new dimension of dignity, equality, and liberty. The document drafted at the end of the meeting made additional points, stating, "The January War began when our grandfathers and grandmothers were first subjected to slavery . . . For centuries, a war of annihilation has been carried out against the peoples native to this land, with no truce or agreement, with no sign of peace or compassion, with no request for pardon on the part of the conquerors, nor redress for the wrongs done." The most tragic aspect of the situation is that their dignity has been trampled underfoot: ". . . nothing is more painful than that we are not taken into account . . . we are persons." They continue, saying that now they know, "that one can die by, and for, a life in which we truly love and respect ourselves."

The insurrection in the highlands was born from a reality without hope. Six months after the beginning of the conflict, with a fragile truce in effect, with the Mexican government in a position of strength, the dialogue between the Zapatistas and the government was interrupted because the system's offers were not concrete, viable, or responsible, and the price demanded was the total surrender of the EZLN. Despite all of this, the people say the Zapatista War is here to stay. The indigenous people are ready to die. And, far from defending the nobility of the human condition, the neoliberal government of Carlos Salinas de Gortari — which is out preaching in other Latin American countries what it doesn't practice at home — furtively supports discrimination and the denial of rights to the Indios, and engenders poverty and contempt for the dignity of the ethnic peoples who are, of course, excluded from plans for developing the country. The human supply is so overabundant that the system has more than it needs.

The balance sheet of the Unfinished War shows the following: In answer to the Zapatista uprising, the National Army counterattacked and hundreds died in those confrontations (the government minimized these figures); a large number of civilian noncombatants also died. In addition, countless suspects were taken prisoner by the federal army, which carried out summary executions, torture and repression, clandestine burials, machine-gun attacks in populated areas, and an assault on a medical center run by Catholic nuns. In the first days of June, reminding us of what has happened in Bosnia, soldiers in one of the reserve units of the municipality of Altamirano raped several indigenous women; no investigation was initiated by the authorities. Despite the truce, the Mexican army continues to harass the civilian population, as well as national and foreign journalists (Irish correspondent Michael McCaughan, for example). Violation of the most basic human rights abounds in Chiapas, in an atmosphere of lawlessness.

The Fighting Kingdoms

What is also significant about this bellicose encounter is the emerging war of symbols, principles, and goals. In the first place, there is the confrontation between unequal and mismatched forces: the Zapatista Army, made up of the ragged, undernourished, and barefoot, bearing wooden guns, the faceless and the voiceless, pitted against a professional army like the armed forces of Mexico, well-equipped, naturally, with all the latest weapons. Then, there is the confrontation between two designs for living: the indigenous way of *being* and *fulfillment,* and the neoliberal way of *possession* and *power;* the indigenous way with its foundation in a cosmogonic, balanced, and magic world, a just life and liberty for all, opposite the Mexican plutocracy, with its political and economic system based on amassing goods and property for some, while leaving only poverty, injustice, and death for the rest of the population. A society without democracy.

The EZLN's act of burning the archives in the municipal offices of San Cristóbal de las Casas — where hundreds and hundreds of petitions and demands for justice, land, rights never granted, falsified property records, and unfinished legal actions were amassed — was not an act of vandalism, as the authorities tried to define it. It was a symbolic act: the EZLN set fire to the lies, robbery, oppression, and cynicism of the system, as represented by City Hall. It was an act of purification. In the same way, the Zapatistas opened jails and released prisoners, the majority of whom were victims of unjust judicial proceedings, which had been tainted by bribery or consigned to oblivion, or they were defendants whose bodies were marked by the brutality of the police. All of this was carried out under the symbol of liberty.

The Mexican government has not understood, nor does it want to understand the acts of this war (which have transcended our borders), the symbolic language of the ethnic peoples, or the magnitude of the problem. The peace dialogue was suspended

196

by the government commissioner; the political parties did not involve themselves, so as not to lose votes in the presidential elections. The only hope remaining is for Mexican society and its democratic organizations to become supporters and guardians of the indigenous demands.

The Indigenous World and Poets

Since childhood, the writers and poets of Chiapas — Rosario Castellanos, Jaime Sabines, Eraclio Zepeda, and myself, among others — have been witnesses to the discrimination, injustice, and exploitation perpetrated against the Indios of the area. At the same time, we have absorbed the influence of their magic and mythical world, which is consequently reflected in our works. In my own case, I share the ideas of the Mayas of the region where I was born, who consider myth to be an elemental instrument with which to interpret reality, enrich essential experience, and contemplate the existential abyss. For the past several years, my poetry has attempted to unleash a mythic energy and awaken the hidden power of early times; like the people of the indigenous world, I believe that the poetic act expresses a paramount human need to connect ourselves to the universe. In no way is my intention to exploit folklore, indigenous ways, or religious beliefs. I want to experiment with poetry of mythic potentiality, a frank and expansive method of reality that reconciles the individual esthetic need with the ethical collective demand.

BP

NO ONE IS LIVING NOW IN MY COUNTRY

Juan Bañuelos

*For the tortured and assassinated
Indios and campesinos*

Imprisoned country

Turbulent
Clamoring
Grieving

It's not the light

It's the smoke that awakens
with the viscera of dust in its hands

It's the rotten rust exhaled
by the disappeared

It's the children who play with skeletons

It's the moon that can discern
all those tortured by their own terror

And on the edges of eyelids
ulcers of hunger

                    Suddenly
        our language

        spits out
        the gravediggers' liquor

        assassins shout
        through the anus

    obsidian winds sweep away
    the saltpeter the haze the red vapor
    of the massacre

    the last second preceding
    enlightenment

    Let the sun set itself in motion
    Let the heavens never again fall upon the earth

    widows scream
    sheltering our foreheads

    with thin mouths
    and the dead eye of the moon

                        The hummingbird's egg:
                        an aurora borealis

    There is a faraway country so turbulent
    so great   And yet again so far

BP

IT COMES FROM AFAR
Eraclio Zepeda

"WHEN THE FLOODWATERS RISE, KNOCKING DOWN houses, and the river overflows, dragging everything along with it, it means it's been raining up in the mountains for days without us knowing," Don Valentín Espinosa said to me.

We'd been talking about how it could be that suddenly war had come to these lands.

And we began to recount all the evil things they've done, and we've done, to the Indians. From the very beginning, when we started off in Spanish, we gave it to them good and hard, no holding back, no pity. If they had good land, we took it. If their land lay alongside a river whose currents were easy to navigate, it was ours. For them, the hillside and the rocky ground. So what if their land was inherited from their grandfathers — our fathers took it away!

"The little bit we left for them was used for growing things we needed; and we paid — *if* we paid — whatever we felt like paying them."

"But that was a long time ago, Don Valentín."

"A long time for us. For them it was only yesterday; it's still an open wound."

I sat there looking at the church, the government buildings and the plaza, all made of finely worked stone. And I thought about the hands that had carved them.

"You can see their hand in everything. Make no mistake," said Don Valentín.

And I sat there thinking about everything I'd been familiar with since childhood: the roads, bridges, dams, wells, foundations, houses. And in everything I perceived the Indians' hand.

"And where do they live?" asked Don Valentín.

"Far away from everything they made," I replied.

"And where do they die?"

"Anywhere. Of anything."

"And why are you surprised?" he asked again.

"Surprised?"

"At what you're seeing . . . ," and Don Valentín lifted his arm to describe the world with his hand.

It was then that we saw them, from the brand-new rubber boots to the new caps, knapsacks on their backs, bodies in uniform, guns in hand, spears in the hands of other compañeros, determined faces under the caps.

"Where are you going?" a woman asked them.

"To war," answered a boy, adjusting his backpack.

"Against who?"

"Against time," replied an old man, tying on the tip of his spear.

"Why war, Don Valentín?" I wanted to know.

"That comes from afar. When the river rises, it means a flood has been building in the mountains for a long, long time."

SMA

La gente tiene hambre. La gente tiene frío.
Los ricos han robado la tierra.
Los ricos han robado la libertad.
La gente exige justícia. De otra manera Revolución.

The people are hungry. The people are cold.
The rich have stolen the land.
The rich have stolen freedom.
The people demand justice. Otherwise, Revolution.

AN EXPRESSION OF PROFOUND GRATITUDE

Leslie Marmon Silko

THIS IS NO NEW WAR. THIS WAR HAS A FIVE-hundred-year history. This is the same war of resistance that the indigenous people of the Americas have never ceased to fight. We are all part of the old stories. Whether we know the stories or not, the stories know about us. From time immemorial, the old stories encompass all events, past and future. The spirits of the ancestors cry out for justice. Their voices are louder now. The mountains shake and fall, the hurricane winds scour the earth, fire and flood engulf the cities as the ancestor spirits announce the time that will return.

Human beings also are natural forces of the Earth. There will be no peace in the Americas until there is justice for the Earth and her children.

In 1980, I became interested in the work of certain archaeologists who were studying the ancient astronomical observatories and the astronomical knowledge that the tribal people of the Americas had possessed long before the arrival of the Europeans. I read about the great culture of the Maya people who had invented the zero and who had performed sophisticated mathematical calculations so that they could predict the positions of the planets and the stars. What interested me about the Mayas was their notion of time; they believed time was a living being that had a personality, a sort of identity. Time was alive and might pass but time did not die; moreover, the days and weeks eventually would return.

Since the days eventually returned, the Maya believed it was possible to know the future if one understood the identities or "souls" of the days from their last appearance among humans. Certain people in touch with the spirits knew the days, weeks, months, and years intimately, and could say exactly whether the days to come were peaceful, full of plenty, or menacing and on the brink of disaster. The Maya people kept track of the days, and weeks, and months, and years in extensive almanacs.

The Maya people made beautiful paper and they had libraries, as the Aztec people had libraries, but Bishop Landa and the Spaniards burned hundreds of thousands of the books. Fragments remain of only three of the Maya almanacs; they are all incomplete. The "codexes" as they are called, are named for the cities where the fragments were located: Madrid, Dresden, and Paris.

I have always been interested in theories of time other than linear time. I don't understand it very well, but I find the theory of curvature in space-time very exciting, and I also love what happens to time when subatomic particles begin bouncing off one another. I love how these particles signal one another or "know" at a speed faster than that of light.

My interest in time comes from my childhood with the old-time people who had radically different views of the universe and reality. For the old-time people, time was not a series of ticks of a clock, one following the other. For the old-time people, time was round — like a tortilla; time had specific moments and specific locations so that the beloved ancestors who had passed on were not annihilated by death, but only relocated to the place called Cliff House. At Cliff House, people continued as they had always been, although only spirits and not living humans can travel freely over this tortilla of time. All times go on existing side by side for all eternity. No moment is lost or destroyed. There are no future times or past times; there are *always all* the times, which differ slightly, as the locations on the tortilla differ slightly. The past and the future are the same because they exist only in the "present" of our imaginations. We can only think and speak in the present, but as we do it is becoming the past, which is always present and which always contains the future encoded in it. Without clocks or calendars we see only the succession of the days, some longer, some shorter, some hotter, some colder; but the succession is cyclic. Without calendars and clocks, the process of "aging" becomes a process of changing: the infant changes; the flower changes; the changes continue relentlessly. Nothing is lost, left behind, or destroyed. It is only changed.

I began thinking about the ancient Maya almanacs and how they had predicted, down to the exact day, the arrival of Cortés. Modern scientists who are envious of ancient Mayan mathematicians call their accurate prediction of the European arrival a "coincidence." I already knew that among the tribal people there were those who could "see" what was happening great distances away.

All the Native American tribes have prophecies that predicted the invasion by the Europeans; but the prophecies also say that all things European will gradually disappear from the Americas.

MY TRIBE
Alberto Blanco

The earth is the same
  the sky is other.
The sky is the same
  the earth is other.

From lake to lake
from forest to forest:
Which one is my tribe?
— I ask myself —
Which one is my home?

Maybe I belong to the tribe
of those who have no tribe;
or the tribe of black sheep;
or a tribe whose ancestors come from the future:
a tribe which has yet to arrive.

But if I must belong to some tribe
— I tell myself —
let it be a big one
let it be a strong one
a tribe where no one

remains outside of the tribe,
where everyone,
all and always
has their sacred place.

I'm not talking about a human tribe.
I'm not talking about a planetary tribe.
And I'm not talking about a universal tribe, either.

I'm talking about a tribe that you can't talk about.

A tribe that has always existed
but whose existence has yet to be proven.

A tribe that has never existed
but whose existence
we could prove right now.

EK

GALLOPING INTO THE FUTURE

Antonio García de León

THE ENORMOUS PARADOX OF HISTORIC TIME/SPACE and the way it works on great persons is largely the product of an inexhaustible popular imagination, one that never stops adorning, to its current taste, upon the founding myths of the past. Emiliano Zapata is alive, today more than ever, seventy-five years after his first death, with new attributes conferred on him by the accelerated history of recent days. He refuses to remain in his tomb, or in the tomb of the past to which the *archaic modernizers* of the present wish to relegate him with their attempts to erase him from official history and to portray this new wave of protest against the Salinista version of Article 27 as mere sterile nostalgia for the past, a simplistic longing for the restoration of a failed utopia.

It's difficult for us to understand, given the decrepit and narrow views of those in power, that this time we really *are* seeing a new campesino movement that is part of a generalized awakening. That we are the fortunate witnesses of a fresh popular wind that is blowing from the fields into the city, created and fostered by the Zapata who was recently reborn in the jungles and mountains of the far South. It's hard to grasp that there are viable alternatives being offered to us by the people of the hoe, the plow, and the pick-axe, that Zapata is galloping into the Zócalo on a horse of the future, groomed and fed by the hope for profound change that has arisen with these recent and sudden events.

The one whom we now remember in an unusual scene of hope is not the old Zapata of the land, of those campesinos of Morelos who, according to Womack, made a revolution because they didn't want to change. No, this is a Zapata who was forged in the collective need for change that has tensed and shaken Mexican society in recent months. And while he returns along with the old, millennial, collective dream of campesinos, this Zapata is somewhat different: this time he's directing his troops against the fortress of arbitrary power — which *does* have a lot in common with a past cabinet of "scientists" that, in 1910, after repeated frauds, thought of itself as part of the First World and whose project for national salvation depended on the trust they placed in foreign investors and on their total contempt for small producers.

This new Zapata has strong support among the urban and educated classes, and has become modern, a privatizer even: he wants a country where the political decisions are not concentrated in a small, secret section of the State apparatus, a country where the dark catacombs of the electoral polls would be opened and turned over to the true private interests — civil society, the heir to Madero's old dream which has as much relevance today as it did in 1910: *Effective suffrage, no reelection.*

His renovated armies enter the city today, as in 1915, demanding a modern agrarian project, steeped in a utopian vision of a fraternal, multicultural, multiethnic nation of tolerance and respect. They arrive loudly demanding their own place in progress and modernity. Because this movement no longer wishes to support the weight of perverse state tutelage, and no longer understands the old language of bureaucratic labyrinths — the language of promises and "agreements" which is the modern mask of the ancient betrayal. Because it has left behind the old, timid leadership who were getting fat "representing" the campesinos before the state, and who are still there, stuck to the teats of the budget and trying to impede change because the ones they represented now refuse to obey them and have come to inaugurate a new century, demanding the true modernization of this country. And all of the "solidarity committees," and the "300 pesos per hectare from Procampo," and all of the bribes handed out for the votes of "those who have less" put together won't suffice to stem this avalanche.

This surprising tide has its most recent origin in the extensive campesino movement of the seventies and eighties, inspired by Zapata and the date of his first death. In its extension, and in spite of its previous apparent defeat — or its domestication in the Permanent Agrarian Council (CAP) — it succeeded in exposing the figurehead nature of the old official center, the fragile rural prop for the pacts and the scanty social programs of exclusive neoliberalism *a la Mexicana*. The most recent apparent death of Zapata was triumphantly crystallized in the reform of Article 27 — the law of January 1992 — which was like a giant pill to be swallowed by the majority of official and independent organizations, whose opinion was left in the margins of the text, making it anything but definitive.

Today it is said, with some truth, that the original Article 27 was dead and didn't respond to the needs of the present, or that the new law that allows the campesinos to sell, rent, or share their land with private investors will bring an end to the scarcity of investment in the countryside and will stimulate the individual responsibilities of rural producers. The better part of the dream of the nineteenth-century liberals and of the "scientists" of the Porfiriato — a past prior to that evoked by those nostalgic for the original Article 27 — would at last have its proper realization. But less is said, or it is simply hidden, about what this implies: the abrupt cancellation of the right of campesinos to the land, the old motor — like it or not — of Mexico's rural history since colonial times. Also omitted is the implicit protection that the reform gives to those who maintain their power by relations of servitude, *caciquismo,* or exploitation, structures that capitalist development and the old regime have generated or recycled. In summary, what is hidden is the legal support that the law gives for the formation of new *latifundios* [large landed estates] by stock investment or that, if investors or abundance don't arrive, the campesinos will be divested of their patrimony in favor of new, unjust concentrations of land and resources.

Ostensibly, the reform gives *ejido*-members the right to choose between selling their land or maintaining it as communal property. To say this much does not recognize the context of crisis and economic pressure which makes this so-called "option" obsolete: the devastation caused by economic policies aimed at the productive sector, benefiting intermediary agents and speculators. It does not mention that the idea of land as commodity would end up replacing the old, but essential concept of earth as mother, and our inalienable patrimony to live from her. It evokes a crisis of self-sufficiency (one which began in 1970 but which has been sharpened to an extreme by current policy) to expect that Mexican campesinos — abandoned to their fate by a delirious neoliberalism — will *compete* with subsidized, modern U. S. producers. What also remains concealed is how the presidency rejected the concrete proposals of the majority of the organizations of the CAP, and how it threatened and bribed legislators for the approval of this law, with no legitimate foundation nor sufficient discussion with the affected sectors of the population. The law was basically approved — as were the Vacant Land laws of the Porfiriato — to make the national agrarian structure compatible with powerful foreign interests, an unequal and increasingly unjust effort which today is called "globalization." If the Salinista reform had been the product of a consensus, as some functionaries asserted, and not merely the imposition of a reform suggested by the World Bank in 1988, it would not be rejected by a majority of the campesino organizations now, as it is being implemented. To the contrary, today there is a general sense in the countryside that it is necessary to reverse, with the force of a civil mobilization, the Salinista reform of Article 27: not in order to return to the past, to the old corporatist, tutelary regime that shamelessly defended the power mongers, but rather, so that a new reform would result from a consensus — legitimate power arising from the popular will. Because in this country, as Madero and Zapata pleaded, there must be elections, referendums, and plebiscites: to enable legitimate power to arise from the popular will and not from fraud, such decisions as the reforms to Article 27 and entry into the Free Trade Agreement must be put to discussion.

The fact is that the collective dream, the most powerful imagining of *México profundo* ["deep" Mexico], has not disappeared — as we'd all believed up until December 31, 1993 — it had simply taken refuge for years in the jungle, in the settlements and valleys, among the ordinary people, forgotten by politics and high-level agreements. It was only the latent dignity maintained there by those who, for centuries, cultivated it in their assemblies and who lovingly placed it in the body of the one whom their enemies had repeatedly betrayed and murdered.

Because today the campesinos demand a complete reform: one which encompasses economic modernization while facilitating an alliance between members of *ejidos*, and communal and private landowners (all under attack by current economic policy); a profound reform accompanied by a new social democratic pact in which everyone participates, not just fancy words emptied of meaning by a corrupt and elitist regime; a reform not limited to the countryside but directed at building a new nation, a project for restoring the republic — whose entrance into the global economic concert would be firm and lasting and would not imply, as it has until now, the scandalous and authoritarian surrender of sovereignty to large international financial interests.

Those who dream with the Porfiriano past, in the sense that they believe the future of Mexico lies exclusively in the Stock Exchange or in the confidence of the great foreign speculators, are once again, as in 1910, being handed an injunction by a youthful and vigorous civil society which pays homage, with its action and its newly won political space, to the immortal utopian dreamer from Anenecuilco — he who contemplates us from the depths of the past/future with eyes full of hope for democracy, justice, and peace with dignity.

CR

QUE VIVA MÉXICO

by Ronnie Burk

> Here they are back again, these barbarian shadows faced like
> a numbered dollar. See them gnawing stones bearing shame
> on their brow, gnawing the earth which is eager to dissolve
> them, gnawing and infecting men to their very core.
>
> *from "Air Mexicain"*
> *— by Benjamin Péret*

THE MEXICAN REVOLUTION OF 1910, ALTHOUGH
emphatically anti-imperialist in spirit, capitulated early on to
its petty-bourgeoise leadership. But the face of the revolution
would remain an indigenous one. At the time when Europe was
preparing for the First World War, in contrast to the prevailing
oppressive forces of international militarism and Western capitalist degradation, Mexico's revolution cleared the way for
the historic possibility of masses of people to collectively participate in the spirit of "*tierra y libertad*." Miners, railroad and oil
refinery workers, campesinos, *vaqueros,* Indios, all revolted
against the tyrannical forces of a thoroughly corrupt dictator-
ship. Seizing haciendas, destroying churches, taking control
of factories, waging strikes, the first People's Revolution of the

century set off a chain reaction that would reverberate around the globe.

José Guadalupe Posada was the Mexican Revolution's greatest artist. A precursor of black humor, vehemently anticlerical, he went so far as to illustrate the assassination of a priest. His malodorous zest for violence, the freakish, and the bizarre animated the pages of broadsides and the popular press of his day. With his caricatures of fat-cat capitalist *burguesas,* yanquí imperialists, emaciated beggars, stiletto-wielding corseted *damas,* and dancing skeletons, Posada's comically derisive art informed masses of Mexicanos of the foibles and corruptions of the Porfiriato. Of Indian parentage, Posada's class allegiances made him the most popular of peoples' artists, and he continues to inspire revolutionary artists the world over.

The genius of Mexico's indigenous world civilization was the lodestone that drew so many of Europe's most radical and far-reaching artists, intellectuals, and visionaries during the last phase of Mexico's epoch-making revolution. During the 1930s, the poet Antonin Artaud was one of the first to make the voyage to the Land of the Mountain of Signs. He arrived announcing that Europe was dead and only Mexico could contain the seeds of a New Civilization. Partaking of the peyote rites of the Tarahumara of Chihuahua, Artaud confirmed what so many would intuit — that in the ritual life of the Native people of Mexico could be found the key to the concretism of the waking dream. The painters Remedios Varo and Leonora Carrington also came to Mexico, fleeing the horrors of the Second World War, and stayed to accomplish their greatest work. The poet Benjamin Péret, kicked out of Brazil for communist agitation, joined Remedios and lived in Mexico for seven years. During his stay he translated the Mayan Sacred Book, the *Chilam Balam,* into French and upon returning to Paris wrote his magnificent long poem, *Air Mexicain.*

Visiting in 1938, André Breton pronounced that Mexico was the surrealist place, *par excellence.* Drawn into that constellation of artists so dear to contemporary Mexicanos — Diego Rivera, Frida Kahlo, Lupe Marin, Nahui Ollin — Breton encountered the painting of Frida Kahlo and proclaimed her a surrealist, a term she rejected, arguing that she did not paint dreams. To the radical theoretician, Kahlo had all the objective appearances of an authentic surrealist, but to the painter and to her fellow countrymen she was — in her art as much as in her dress, her gender identification, her loves, and her passionate nationalism and strong anti-imperialist politics — puro Mexicana. For it was her *mestizaje* that defined her, both politically and artistically. And like Posada before her, Kahlo exemplified for Breton that Mexico was indeed surrealist, in art *and* revolution.

Others would make their way across the Atlantic to partake of Mexico, for example, the Russian filmmaker Sergei Eisenstein whose unfinished masterwork, *Que Viva México*, a tribute to *la raza morena,* has long been acknowledged as a milestone of epic cinema. And who could forget Sylvia Pinal as La Diabla in Luis Buñuel's *Simon Desierto?* But of all the remarkable figures to arrive, undoubtedly the greatest was Leon Trotsky, leader, military strategist, and historian of the October Revolution. Invited by the Mexican president, Lázaro Cárdenas as a guest of the government (due in large part to the influence of Diego Rivera), Trotsky arrived in Mexico to find himself at odds with Cárdenas's supporters, including the Confederation of Mexican Workers, which was a Stalinist stronghold — a fact that would lead to tragic consequences. President Cárdenas was busy expropriating Mexico's oil and railway systems from British and U.S. interests, and had to distance himself from the Bolshevik revolutionary. Nonetheless, he and his wife Natalia Sedova found refuge under the auspices of Mexico's nationalist revolution. Amid threats, accusations, bad press, and the constant presence of police guards, Leon Trotsky maintained a rigorous schedule of writing, reading, discussing, and directing the Fourth International. During André Breton's visit, Trotsky collaborated with the poet on a manifesto, "Towards a Free Revolutionary Art," highly critical of the conditions of the artist in both the Stalinist and the reactionary bourgeois state. Since the collapse of the Soviet state, Trotsky's writings, in particular his theory of permanent revolution (on the permanent nature of the world revolution, i.e., international proletarianism), have demonstrated a prescience that cannot be discounted. Recent events confirm that Mexico's revolutionary character is very much in keeping with Trotsky's formulations. From his "Fourteen Propositions on the Permanent Revolution":

> 2. With regard to the countries with a belated bourgeois development, especially the colonial and semi-colonial countries, the theory of permanent revolution signifies that the complete and genuine solution of their tasks, *democratic and national emancipation*, is conceivable only through the dictatorship of the proletariat as the leader of the subjugated nation, above all its peasant masses.

The EZLN's call for regional autonomy and economic and social democracy could transform the nation. For, contrary to apologists such as Bill Clinton and Al Gore, dictatorships are not reformed, dictatorships are overthrown, and the initial Peoples' Revolution of this century may yet find its way to completion. The conditions exist in Mexico for a true workers' state to emerge out of the ongoing crisis. At the end of this mad century of revolutions, Mexico might very well show the world how it's done.

MEXICO 1994:
THE RUINS OF THE FUTURE
Mongo Sánchez Lira and Rogelio Villarreal

I. TWO MINUTES BEFORE THE ELECTIONS

There is None so Deaf as He Who Will Not Hear

We all know that many North American leftist intellectuals have a tendency to romanticize the violent social processes south of the border. It seems that, for them, we will always be curious and exotic subjects in need of redemption. Take the case of Cuba, a nation — and notion — that for a good part of them still represents a paradigm of dignity, and even democracy — can you believe it? Socialists immersed in the American Way of Life adamantly and punctually point out the errors of their own government, with its constant disregard of human rights in Cuba and other countries but, along with many of their Latin

American fellow-believers, when dealing with governments or *caudillo*-style leaders (which aren't the same thing) cynically clothed in revolutionary gear, their compliance is irritating. Their partiality makes them incapable of acknowledging that the Cuban people suffer hunger and scarcity not just because of the famous embargo, but rather due to the ineptitude and messianic stupidity of their highest leader — the world's most costly economist — and the uncritical, unconditional servility of his governmental apparatus. Testimonies and historical examples are of no avail; one after another the solidarity caravans leave with their food, medicine and fuel, vainly attempting to supply what Castro's regime cannot provide for the population. The example of Sandinista Nicaragua speaks for itself: the people themselves turned their backs once the revolutionaries, dizzy with power, foolishly lost the opportunity they'd won through years of struggle and bloodshed. Nevertheless, the North American left, as well as the left of our countries, continued to stubbornly support the mythic Sandinistas while it blamed — and not without reason — the gringo government for interventionism.

Landscape After the Battle

Subcomandante Marcos, the university-educated *mestizo*, spokesperson for the Zapatista National Liberation Army, is a guerrilla hero able to "inspire an insane love" in the envoy from *Vanity Fair* — well, not only in her — and to fascinate locals and foreigners alike. A charismatic and complex personality, he's been at the center of the tornado that has lashed at Mexico since the first of January. Lucid, enigmatic, serene, sensationalist, gallant, virile, romantic, sometimes almost kitschy and vain (like a hero in a gringo movie!), he is not infrequently accurate in his judgment and in his crude diagnosis of the sick body of the country. Leader of the first post-Communist revolution (in the words of the accommodating Carlos Fuentes) or vulgar and loquacious in the extreme (as he was described early on by the increasingly intolerant and authoritarian Octavio Paz), the prolific, faceless writer hidden behind the ski mask of the Subcomandante shook and divided public opinion with his brilliant handling of the media. Never before had a Latin American guerrilla movement so clearly established its distance from other pro-Cuban or Maoist movements, with no pretext of any attempt to take power, but rather that of functioning to guarantee the transition to a democratic government (allowing full justification for their armed uprising, given the obvious conditions of misery and humiliation of the indigenous people of southeastern Mexico). Sympathy for the leader and for the Zapatista movement quickly turned into mythification — and not without a guilty conscience: they are the poor Indians of Mexico, oppressed since time immemorial, thus they are *more* Mexican, *ergo*, they are right: only they understand dignity and how to regain it. This reasoning hindered the enlightened middle class from understanding why thousands of other indigenous people had rejected and even repudiated the armed struggle chosen by the rebels, a fact that caused friction and confrontations that the Mexican Left didn't wish to understand. A good example: the frustration of disconcerted members of the National Autonomous University Student Council, supposedly democratic but in reality rigid and intolerant, obliged to hand over blankets and food supplies to Indians of a *non*-Zapatista town. Another example: the enthusiastic chronicles of many journalists in democratic dailies like *La Jornada*, for whom the indigenous people who aren't with *el Sup* are necessarily manipulated by ranchers and PRI functionaries.

Off with the Masks

A few weeks before the elections, the horizon is uncertain, dark and unpredictable, but everyone knows that our late, much-publicized arrival at First World modernity is only a post-modern facade designed by the country's new leadership, those installed in the increasingly narrow and petulant summit of power — all graduates from prestigious North American universities, *of course*. Mexico is struggling with an ancestral division of classes — and the markings are not only economic, but racial — aggravated during the last presidential term by the hyperconcentration of capital in the hands of a few families, constantly increasing unemployment, and an exasperating loss of buying power. More than anything, the much-touted modernization has consisted of a minimal opening of the media, until very recently controlled — in a manner more feudal than monopolistic — almost entirely by the Televisa consortium, openly in league with the government. Nevertheless, this opening, needed to project an international image of stability and progress — and to a great degree, inevitable given the accelerating world evolution of the means of communication — has come with some consequences that are escaping government control. Television via satellite, fax machines, the international newspapers and magazines, as well as imported TV series carried by local stations — like "The Simpsons," to cite one example — have modified the world vision and the value system of the average Mexican, allowing him or her to compare, albeit in an indirect and subjective way, the quality of their own environment and social system with those of other countries. The same phenomenon, incidentally, that precipitated the collapse of the Berlin Wall and is now provoking the fall of Fidel Castro.

The Coup Announced (or "*como México no hay dos . . .*")

Civil society has been shaken from its traditional lethargy in recent years by events such as the gas explosions at a Pemex plant in San Juanico in 1984, the earthquake of 1985, the cynical electoral fraud of 1988, the terrible explosion of gasoline which had leaked into the public sewer system in Guadalajara in 1992, and the surprising outbreak of the war in Chiapas.[1] The government, plagued by corruption and inefficiency, has been largely supplanted on these occasions by the spontaneous action of the population which has developed a new critical edge in confronting the lies of the powerful (supported in large measure by an increasingly popular written press, counterpart to the general discrediting of televised information), and with a growing self-consciousness of its own power, its rights and its organizational abilities that far exceed the methods for control of the masses used until now by the ruling class. The scarce credibility of the party in power, eroded by several decades of unfulfilled promises, has entered into full bankruptcy brought about by an internal war that the old mask of revolutionary unity is no longer able to maintain. Dinosaurs and modernizers, traditional politicians and technocratic yuppies — distanced from the people and clinging fiercely to what each one of them believes is the only possible way to continue in power — struggle for control of the wheel with an alarming profusion of low blows.

The Three Disgraces (or, Watching in Hope)

Before the terrified eyes of public opinion, the murders of Cardenal Posadas and of the PRI presidential candidate, Luis Donaldo Colosio Murrieta, appear to be a dark settling of accounts in the factional struggles. To the long and unpunished chain of kidnappings of businessmen and bankers (the most recent: Harp Helú and Angel Lozada, two of the richest men of the country and the world, *dixit Forbes*) presumably perpetrated

[1] In November of 1984, there was a tremendous explosion of giant gas storage tanks on the outskirts of Mexico City. Another explosion in April 1992, this time due to leaking gas in the public drainage system of Guadalajara, sent entire streets flying. In both cases there were many people killed and Pemex, a state-owned producer and distributor of petroleum, has been implicated for negligent behavior.

by ex-policemen or drug dealers or terrorists or (you name it), can be added a no shorter list — in ways that break the national record — of journalists and militant politicians murdered, disappeared, or "accidented" in more than suspicious circumstances throughout the length and breadth of this country in these past six years. The systematic imprisonment of high-ranking police chiefs, scapegoat-style, rather than appeasing exasperated public opinion, has only made more evident the grotesque degree of cynicism and corruption that reigns among the forces of law and order, which are profoundly infiltrated by narco-trafficking, as some of its leaders have openly confessed. The discredit of the police forces and the popular indignation against them is such that in recent months the lynching of police and burning of patrol cars has abounded in the capital as well as in all the states of the republic.

The average citizen, skeptical of authority, exhibits a kind of malaise with respect to the electoral contest, despite the repeated official and officious promise that these will be the cleanest elections in our history. A political campaign, based more on the dubious personalities of the candidates than on their vague and little-discussed programs for governing, is a confrontation between three parties with real possibilities for the possession of the presidency (PRI, PAN, PRD) and some four or five others (PT, PFCRN, PARM and the new Green Party) with no hopes — whether for lack of followers or because they are simply satellites directed by the PRI, with the obvious aim of completely confusing the electorate and subtracting votes from the big three.

The party of the left (PRD), unimaginative, weighted down by old dogmatic and messianic traditions, headed by Cuauhtémoc Cárdenas — son of the most popular of the PRI ex-presidents, himself an ex-Priista, with marked indigenous features, a bitter grimace, monotone voice, and limited mental agility — has the support of a good number of intellectuals and the poorest classes of the country. The PAN, the rightist party, intolerant and reactionary, headed by Diego Fernández de Cevallos — a small-town macho, lawyer, and son of large land-owners, with the aspect and attitude of a Spanish conquistador — is supported by the upper-middle class, the so-called "decent folk," white and Catholic, convinced of the not-so-Christian virtues of free enterprise and neoliberal economics. And the eternal PRI, divided and discredited in public opinion, with Ernesto Zedillo Ponce de León — a last-minute candidate, gray bureaucrat with a false and facile smile, obedient to the presidential slogans, with scant charisma. These are the options that face the electorate. The physical and psychological characteristics of the three candidates represent, in comic caricature, the virtues and defects of the primary ethnic types of our country. Cárdenas: the stubbornness and self-absorption of the indigenous; Cevallos: the haughty and arrogant authoritarianism of the Spaniard; Zedillo: the hypocritical prudence of the *mestizo*, of the *ladino*. The Three Wise Men of a postmodern political ethno-nightmare.

It is clear that many of the votes cast will have a negative character. That is, there will be those who vote for the PAN or the PRD simply because they're sick of the PRI and not because they believe these parties to be good choices for the government. Others will vote for the PRI from fear of change, applying the old saying, "better a known evil than an unknown good," or simply — and this above all in the most backward rural areas — out of ignorance or fear of reprisal. In this way, a superficially modernized country with a pitiful operetta democracy, a backward productive base, drowning in a culture of corruption and inefficiency and with a ruling class that has lost political control, moves along the inevitable path of the Free Trade Agreement and the consequent invasion of products from the First World, with superior quality and better prices to cheer the few who have the power to buy.

These Ruins You See

The situation in Chiapas is still at a desperate impasse while the rest of the country bleeds, falls apart, and convulses from top to bottom, as the news and leading journalists point out: every day more children are born without brains in the north (our Chernobyl); every day there are more workers without jobs and campesinos without land (our unemployment insurance); the soccer fanatics celebrate with blood and death the victories and defeats of the national team (our Aztec traditions, brought up to date); insistent rumors refer to Salinas de Gortari and his group remaining in power (our technocratic version of political stability); Zabludovsky and Raúl Velasco — the spokespersons for the radio and television monopolies — openly lie to and manipulate millions of citizens; crime settles into the streets, and police and thieves, distinguishable only by their uniforms, crush the population (haven't we seen this movie?). The glorious Mexican army beats and rapes defenseless indigenous people while the chief of staff denies it (it could be another film by Oliver Stone, right?); about thirty armed guerrilla organizations are lying in wait in different parts of the country *(Apocalypse Now);* crazed adolescents murder their parents and siblings (just like in the United States!); rival factions of Chiapan Indians mutually accuse each other of betraying their (sic) religion, their party, their cause (how do you like that, we're still celebrating the five hundred Years of Conquest); the children in the streets huddle together in sewers to sniff solvents (Disneyland within the reach of everyone); middle-class youths murder prostitutes with the luxury of cruelty *(Taxi Driver);* on the street, people look at each other with distrust (like in New York); a young poet has just been freed from two years of incarceration, accused of Satanism by the PAN government in Guanajuato (remember McCarthy the Inquisitor?).

We live in a frightened country in collapse, hiding the rictus of terror behind a modern plastic mask. The emotional and familial bonds are stretched thin. Parricide and magnicide mark our frustrated arrival in the First World. No one understands anything anymore.

As Johnny Rotten Says (or, Please Put this Message in a Bottle)

Any attempt to explain the dizzying, schizophrenic, and changing Mexican reality is, to say the least, pretentious. Many expect violence throughout the country, convinced that the government will commit electoral fraud again. Marcos and the Zapatistas convoke a tumultuous and enthusiastic National Democratic Convention, which the "distinguished" and accommodating intellectuals, politicians, and functionaries of the *Grupo San Angel* — busy quantifying and qualifying the contenders for the presidency in a friendly atmosphere of good taste — decline to attend, but which brings together thousands of representatives from democratic, campesino, and popular organizations and, of course, dozens of opportunists and yea-sayers — some of them seated, quite self-satisfied, on the presidium. The pages of the newspapers are full of conscientious political analysis that goes nowhere while Mexicans live in anguished uncertainty of the future — an intense anxiety which equalizes in confusion the political analyst, the campesino, and the man on the street. No one can see beyond August 21 [election day]. Television and the press offer up images of death and suffering with extraordinary abundance: from Rwanda to Bosnia, from Argentina to India, from Peru to Chiapas. Our map, practically immaculate before, looks more and more like the bloody rags that swaddle the planet. Perhaps the immediate lesson, so tough and difficult to learn, would be that in these closing years of the century progress is the patrimony of only a few members of a neofeudal society, taking refuge in malls and suburbs while barbarism spreads throughout the rest of the world with an overwhelming force. The punks in the mid-seventies already said it: There is no future. It's true: the idealistic theses which took for granted the generalized progress of humanity seem to have an steadily eroding foundation. Nevertheless, many of us would like to think that things could slowly improve. We still have one hope left: maybe the Martians will come soon.

Mexico City, August 11, 1994
(Ten days before the elections . . .)

II. ONE DAY AFTER: 50 PERCENT? HA HA HA!

And when he woke up, the dinosaur was still there . . .
— *Tito Monterroso*

A faltering Octavio Paz, growing closer to those in power by the minute, curtly affirmed that the August elections were clean, and that the electoral officials — with the malleable and pusillanimous Jorge Carpizo functioning as both secretary of the government and head of the Federal Electoral Institute — could feel proud of their work. A substantial number of intellectuals and "representatives" from civil groups had already affirmed, without blushing, that "fraud exists in all democratic countries," with no mention of the extraordinary magnitude of that which was perpetrated on August 21st. Machiavelli could well have been the sorcerer's apprentice for the immense and perfect machinery that made possible, for the thousandth time, the dismal perpetuation of the ruling party in power: from the "*ratón loco*" and the "merry-go-round" to "*tacos de votos*" and "operation tamale";[2] from the outright robbery of ballot boxes to the indimidation and violence directed against opposition voters, or those who

---

[2] The *"ratón loco"* is when a voter is sent from one polling place to another, in an attempt to discourage him/her from voting. The "merry-go-round" refers to groups of PRI voters who are transported in truckloads to vote at various locations. "Operation tamale" and *"tacos de votos"* are methods used by the PRI to stuff ballot boxes with fraudulent votes.

were simply apathetic; from shaving thousands of voters' names from the official electoral registry to the magic which brought the dead back from the Great Beyond to joyously cast their votes for the Tricolor Party, and finally, of course, the cyber-cosmetic makeover of the results which was carried out in the offices of the government. While it is true that a great number of people voted for the most conservative and retrograde options, the figure of 50 percent which the media and the PRI put forth is madly laughable. Thousands of people cried out in unison in the Zócalo of the capital and in plazas throughout the country: "50 percent? HA HA HA!"

Those who had been dreaming of change awakened to the same nightmare, modernized this time. The PRI strategy produced such good results that it surprised even the party hierarchy itself. The polarization of the two opposition parties — leaving the PRI in the center — the highly-publicized purchase of antiriot tanks, the veiled and subliminal suggestion that chaos would result from a PRD or a PAN victory, the threats from big business and bankers that they would leave the country with their money and everything else, and of course, the guerrilla in Chiapas, weighed heavily on the voters — frightened, conservative, and with no real options.

Confronted with hundreds of international observers, the PRI moderated its deceitful strategies for vote-stealing, applying them with more discretion, and with a preference for remote rural areas with difficult access and an easily manipulated electorate. Meanwhile, in a far-off corner of the Chiapan jungle, the rebels watch through ski masks and wait. . . .

The violence that was expected has not sprung from the masses, but rather from the convulsions that the new, brutal apocalyptic horseman's spurs are causing in the corrupt and cynical beast that is Mexico's governing apparatus. Narcopower has crawled into the government control posts, allying itself with the political class and imposing its new, more savage ways upon the old rulers, as was evident in the flagrant assassination of Francisco Ruiz Massieu, the brand-new head of the PRI parliamentarians and also the link between Salinas and Zedillo, the pragmatists and the technicians.

Mexico will not be the same in the future. Everything has changed, but as Lampedusa said so well, only for everything to remain the same. To the old rulers — voracious capitalists and corrupt politicians — is added a new one, more corrupt, voracious and savage: narcopower. From antidemocracy we move on to narco-democracy. That is our sad modernity.

Back to the Past

The communications media unify the country. The new peons are wearing jeans and Pendleton shirts, and instead of the small, old stores we now have franchises: we can even buy gringo tortillas in the supermarkets! Everywhere, the following scene reproduces itself like a hologram in a house of mirrors: at a cash register, a pretechnological, malnourished Mexican numbly contemplates a computer (that Mystery which will bear him into the future) while some gringo in some part of the network tallies up the profits for the day. Outside of the establishment (McDonald's, Wal-Mart, Seven Eleven, Price Club, you name it), life continues on pretty much the same — just a little more violent. And finally, what's left to say, since here it's always been like the song goes: *la vida no vale nada* [life is worth nothing].

CR

XILOTL
Jack Hirschman

Xihualhuian ollóque yaoyóaque
Come forward, O ballplayers, warriors
you of the rubber and the marigold
I am the skeleton of chocolate
inside the skin of the Red Mirror,
the enchanted head of the people
many times decapitated
bouncing from *milpa* to street
with looted eyes extorted ears
thoughts defrauded by the Scorpion
with more than sixty legs and a tail
packed with decades of poison.

I'm speaking to your hips and
your shoulders, O ballplayers and warriors,
bouncing from one neck to another,
telling over and over — with variations
of lips grimaces cries grumbles and groans —
how the NAFTA New Order is lethal gas
intended to turn our land into a death chamber,
how it is a crusher of the intestines

of squash, a dirty smear of smog, ash
and grated pesos on tortillas to eat and die from,
and the stinking up of the sweet-potato
thighs and the lip-biting flowers.

I'm censing from this pot of rage
on this trivet of stones on a sidestreet
of a Mayanalan slum;
I'm speaking to gums that no longer have teeth
(the PRI has yanked them)
to teeth that no longer have gold
(the PRI has stolen it)
to bones starving under layers of rags,
to rachitic chests, to gangrene, to pneumonia,
to the whole Commune Deficiency System which
the PRI has depleted, poisoned and thrown away
like tripe in a supermercado garbage-can.

The chocolate skeleton from Tenantzingo
to Mescaltepec is exhorting you,
O ballplayers O warriors
Xilotl Xilotl emerging ears of corn
Listen Listen for the movement
of living glyphs and stelae in the jungle
They have embraced They have united
despite the abrasions of injustice and fraud
Listen to the copal's whirling messengers
The Fire opening its mouth The Tree pouring forth
O plume of People's Oil touched by the word
all true men and women live for!

O spurt of flame from the guts of deepest hungers!
O tongue of the Incendiary Serpent,
we will be with you tomorrow when we strike!

MOVABLE EMPIRE
Elva Macías

The sun bathes
irregular rainbows:
vessels of light in the dark jungle.

Everything arrives late in Chiapas,
says Eraclio, *even war.*

We were many and the jungle gave birth,
from her branching womb
from her leafy pubis
they burst forth to the war for bread.

War never sleeps
it's a bridge suspended in the sky.
Archangels cross it,
God's invisible armada.

Where are they marching?
How can it be told
on scraps of old paper?

Trappings improvised in the shadows
artesans braiding leather cartridge belts
joined the revolution in their tongues.

Armies move into formation
there are signs of blood in the water
ash in the wind
sulphur in the fire.

Where are they going?
Bat-men in migration
in search of bread, under a humble cloak.
They've kicked up a storm
hidden, waiting in the *juncia*
that trembles in all of their rituals.

War, tinder among the rocks
and dry leaves, advances
like the fires of April.

They descended
with the secrecy of the mist
that veils Ciudad Real.
For one day they established their movable empire
in the plazas:
Don't leave us alone
five hundred more years.

EK

GLOSSARY

artesanía handmade crafts

Article 27 section of the Mexican Constitution which deals with agrarian reform, altered by President Salinas in 1992, effectively ending land redistribution

burguesas bourgeoisie

cabrón (slang) a macho with no shame

cacique local political boss

Camacho Solís, Manuel former mayor of Mexico City, a PRI party official, acted as Commissioner for Peace and Reconciliation in Chiapas in the government's dialogue with the EZLN

campesino/a man/woman who works the land, peasant

Cárdenas, Cuauhtémoc Left-party (PRD) candidate for president, widely believed to have won the popular vote in 1988 elections

caudillo an individual, supreme leader of a political movement, especially a guerrilla

colonia neighborhood or settlement

Colosio, Luis Donaldo PRI presidential candidate, assassinated in Tijuana in March, 1994

compadre close friend

compañero comrade, companion, friend

Convención Nacional Democrática [National Democratic Convention] convened by the EZLN in August, 1994, a 3-day meeting which brought together intellectuals and activists from social organizations throughout Mexico, it is now the name of the coalition which was formed as a result of the meeting

damas women

ejido collectively held land, awarded in land reforms

expulsados people who have been exiled from their village

foquista advocating a form of guerrilla warfare which involves form-
ing a liberated zone in the mountains, advancing toward the
cities; associated with Ché Guevara

Ganadera ranchers' association

González, Patrocinio former governor of Chiapas, Mexico's Minister
of the Interior who was dismissed during the January uprising

Grupo San Angel a group of intellectuals, an association formed as a
result of the crisis in Chiapas

guerrilla insurgent war

guerrillero/a male/female soldier in an insurgent army

Guardias Blancas [White Guards] armed guards hired by ranchers to
protect their property

hectare a unit of land, approximately 2.5 acres

hermano brother

huipil embroidered blouse

indígena indigenous person

Indios Chiapan term for indigenous people

judiciales federal police

juncia pine needles

la raza morena "the brown race"

ladino person of Spanish descent, or mixed indigenous and Spanish
descent, associated with bourgeoise society

latifundio large estate

latifundista wealthy land-owner

mestizo person of mixed indigenous and European descent

milpa corn field

neoliberalism a free-market, anti-state approach to economics and international relations

norteño/ismo person from the north of Mexico / idiommatic expressions from the north of the country

PAN Right-wing national political party

paraje a piece of land, awarded in land reform

patrón boss

Pemex state-owned Mexican oil company

Plan de Ayala the land reform plan proposed by Emiliano Zapata

Porfirista/Porfiriato refers to the regime of Porfirio Díaz, the dictator who was overthrown by the Mexican Revolution

PRD Center-left, national political party

PRI the political party which has ruled Mexico for 65 years

Solidarity Program national program of rural aid

Tierra y Libertad "Land and Liberty;" Emiliano Zapata's slogan

vaqueros cowboys

zapatismo political ideology, refers to Emiliano Zapata, advocate of land reform and indigenous rights in the Mexican Revolution of 1910

zócalo main square

ILLUSTRATIONS

Notes for "A North American Indigenist View," p. 141

1. On the indigenous ethnography of Chiapas, see James D. Nations, *Population Ecology of the Lancandón Maya* (University Microfilms International, No. GAX79-20363, 1979).
2. An excellent overview will be found in David E. Stannard, *American Holocaust: Columbus and the Conquest of the New World* (Oxford University Press, 1992).
3. Duncan Earl, "Indigenous Identity at the Margin: Zapatismo and Nationalism," *Cultural Survival Quarterly*, vol. 18, no. 1, Spring 1994, p. 27.
4. For details on Zapata's life and politics, see John Womack, *Zapata and the Mexican Revolution*.
5. For background on the PRI's performance in this respect, see George A. Collier, "Roots of the Rebellion in Chiapas," *Cultural Survival Quarterly*, vol. 18, no. 1, Spring 1994.
6. The perspective pertains even among most Euroamerican progressives; see, e.g., Ronald Wright, *Time Among the Maya: Travels in Belize, Guatemala and Mexico* (Viking Press, 1990).
7. The sort of devaluation of the "Other" involved is analyzed well and thoroughly in Albert Memmi, *Colonizer and Colonized* (Beacon Press, 1967); also see Robert Jay Lifton and Eric Markuson, *The Genocidal Mentality: Nazi Holocaust and Nuclear Threat* (Basic Books, 1990).
8. The psychology is well-handled in Stannard, op. cit.
9. Memmi, op. cit., and *Dominated Man* (Beacon Press, 1976).
10. For analysis and discussion, see Frantz Fanon, *The Wretched of the Earth* (Grove Press, 1965).
11. Arturo Santamaría Gómez, "Zapatistas Deliver a Message From 'Deep Mexico,'" *Z Magazine*, vol. 7, no. 3, March 1994, p. 33.
12. Ibid., p. 30.
13. Ibid., p. 33.
14. Interesting, if occasionally reactionary and misleading, observations on these dynamics will be found in Frank Cancian and Peter Brown, "Who Is Rebelling in Chiapas?" *Cultural Survival Quarterly*, vol. 18, no. 1, Spring 1994, pp. 22–25.
15. Santamaría Gómez, op. cit., p. 32.
16. Ibid.
17. Grant D. Jones, *Maya Resistance to Spanish Rule: Time and History on a Colonial Frontier* (University of New Mexico Press, 1989).
18. George Lovell, *Conquest and Survival in Colonial Guatemala: A Historical Geography of the Chuchumatan Highlands*, 1500–1821 (McGill-Queen's University Press, 1985).
19. For elaboration on this point in a related setting, see Paulo Friere, *Pedagogy of the Oppressed* (Herder and Herder, 1972).
20. See Hugh Seton-Watson, *Nations and States: An Inquiry into the Origins*

of Nations and the Politics of Nationalism (Westview Press, 1977); Greg Urban and Joel Sherzer, eds., *Nation-States and Indians in Latin America* (University of Texas Press, 1992).

21. For discussion of the principles of self-determination involved, see S. James Anaya, "The Rights of Indigenous People and International Law in Historical and Contemporary Perspective," in Robert N. Clinton, Nell Jessup Newton, and Monroe E. Price, *American Indian Law: Cases and Materials* (Michie Co., Law Publishers, 1991, pp. 1257–76).

22. For elaboration, see George Manuel, *The Fourth World: An Indian Reality* (The Free Press, 1974).

23. On Guevara, see *The Bolivian Diaries of Che Guevara* (Grove Press, 1968); on Allende, see James Petras and Morris Morely, *The United States and Chile: Imperialism and the Overthrow of the Allende Government* (Monthly Review Press, 1975); on Sendic and the Tupamaros, see Maria Esther Gilio, *The Tupamaro Guerrillas: The Structure and Strategy of an Urban Guerrilla Movement* (Saturday Review Press, 1970); on Castro, see Carlos Franqui, *Family Portrait with Fidel: A Memoir* (Vintage Books, 1985); on the Sandinistas, see Henri Weber, *Nicaragua: The Sandinista Revolution* (Verso Press, 1981); on Sendero Luminoso, see Simon Strong, *Shining Path: Terror and Revolution in Peru* (HarperCollins , 1992); on the FMLN, see Robert Armstrong and Janet Shenk, *El Salvador: The Face of Revolution* (South End Press, 1982); overall, see Sheldon B. Bliss, *Marxist Thought in Latin America* (University of California Press, 1984).

24. David Hemming, *Red Gold: The Conquest of the Brazilian Indians, 1500–1760* (Harvard University Press, 1978).

25. Editors, *Túpac Amaru II* (Lima: n.p., 1976).

26. Bernardo Berdichewsky, *The Araucanian Indian in Chile* (Copenhagen: IWGIA Doc. No. 20, 1975).

27. Evelyn Hu-DeHart, *Yaqui Resistance and Survival* (University of Wisconsin Press, 1984).

28. See Alvin Josephy, Jr., *The Patriot Chiefs* (Viking Press, 1961).

29. On the Pueblo revolt, see Oakah L. Jones, Jr., *Pueblo Warriors and the Spanish Conquest* (University of Oklahoma Press, 1966); on Tecumseh, see David R. Edmunds, *Tecumseh and the Quest for American Indian Leadership* (Little Brown, 1984); on the rest, see Dee Brown, *Bury My Heart at Wounded Knee: An Indian History of the American West* (Little Brown, 1970).

30. Quoted in Santamaría Gómez, op. cit., p. 33.

31. For a succinct exploration, see Evon Z. Vogt, "Possible Sacred Aspects of the Chiapas Rebellion," *Cultural Survival Quarterly*, vol. 18, no. 1, Spring 1994.

32. See James D. Nations, "The Ecology of the Zapatista Revolt," *Cultural Survival Quarterly*, vol. 18, no. 1, Spring 1994.

33. For a good examination of the likely impacts of the NAFTA on the Mayas

of Chiapas, and hence the basis for the Zapatista response, see Gary C. Hufbauer and Jeffrey J. Schott, *NAFTA: An Assessment* (Washington, D.C.: Institute for International Economics, 1993).

34. Those interested in pursuing these matters further might be interested in Evon Z. Vogt's *The Zinacatecos of Mexico: A Modern Maya Way of Life* (Holt, Rinehart and Winston, 1990).

35. Bernard Neitschmann, "World War III," *Cultural Survival Quarterly*, vol. 11, no. 4, Fall 1988.

36. For further background on the conditions precipitating these struggles, see *Indigenous Peoples: A Global Quest for Justice* (Zed Books, 1987).

37. Santamaría Gómez (op. cit., p. 33), points out that there is also indication of Zapatista-type activity in the provinces of Morelos, Chihuahua, Veracruz, Tabasco and San Luis Potosí and that there have been armed actions in Guadalajara and Mexico City. I know from personal experience that ferment among the people along the Yaqui River in Sonora Province is also leading in the same direction.

38. On the Karins and Tamils, see Aga Khan and bin Tabal, op. cit.; on the Euskadi, see Kenneth Medhurst, *The Basques and Catalans*, Minority Rights Support Group No. 9, September 1977; on the Irish, see J. Bowyer Bell, *The Irish Troubles: A Generation of Violence, 1967–1992* (St. Martin's Press, 1993); on the Polisario, see Tony Hodges, *Western Sahara: The Roots of a Desert War* (Lawrence Hill & Co., 1983); on the Papuans, see David Robie, *Blood on Their Banner: Nationalist Struggles in the South Pacific* (Zed Books, 1989).

39. Quoted in Santamaría Gómez, op. cit., p. 33.

40. Neitschmann, op. cit.

41. Santamaría Gómez, op. cit., p. 31.

42. See, e.g., Glenn T. Morris and Ward Churchill, "Between a Rock and a Hard Place: Left-Wing Revolution, Right-Wing Reaction and the Destruction of Indigenous Peoples," *Cultural Survival Quarterly*, vol. 11, no. 3, Fall 1988.

43. See, e.g., Ward Churchill, "False Promises: An Indigenist Critique of Marxist Theory and Practice," *Fourth World Journal*, vol. II, no. 2, Fall 1990. The issue is treated in greater detail, relying on exhaustive case histories, in Walker Connor, *The National Question in Marxist-Leninist Theory and Practice* (Princeton University Press).

44. For discussion, see Connor, op. cit.

45. Santamaría Gómez, *op. cit.*, p. 33.

For a discussion of the agenda of indigenism, how settler populations fit into it, and for further reading, see Ward Churchill, *Struggle for the Land: Indigenous Resistance to Genocide, Ecocide and Expropriation in Contemporary North America* (Common Courage Press, 1993).

CONTRIBUTORS' NOTES

Munda Tostón has a stall in the marketplace in San Cristóbal, Chiapas.

Efraín Bartolomé was born in Ocosingo, Chiapas in 1950. He lives in Mexico City, where he practices psychotherapy. He is the recipient of two National Prizes for Poetry, the Aguascalientes in 1984, and the Universidad de Querétaro in 1987.

Alberto Huerta is associate professor in the Department of Modern and Classical Languages at the University of San Francisco.

Paulina Hermosillo Rodríguez is a photojournalist who has been documenting the social, religious,and cultural movements of Mayan people in Yucatán, Campeche, Tabasco, Quintana Roo, and Chiapas since 1989.

Hortensia Sierra Mancera works as an editor, graphic designer, and photojournalist. She has collaborated in various publications in Mexico.

Elizabeth Luis Díaz is a journalist who specializes in contemporary Mexican literature.

Blanche Petrich is a journalist for *La Jornada* in Mexico. She lives in Mexico City.

Medea Benjamin is the co-director of Global Exchange, an organization devoted to grassroots development and international cooperation. She has worked with various communities and organizations in Mexico for over 20 years, and was part of the first human rights delegation to Chiapas in January, 1994. She is supervisor of the U.S.-Mexico Project for Development.

Xunka Utz'utz'ni lives in San Juan Chamula, Chiapas, where she makes fireworks.

John Ross is a San Francisco/Mexico City-based journalist, poet and author of *Rebellion from the Roots* (Common Courage Press, 1995). He has been covering popular struggle in the Americas since 1957, and is a regular contributer to *The Anderson Valley Advertiser, The Nation,* and *The San Francisco Bay Guardian.*

Guillermo Gómez Peña is an internationally recognized interdisciplinary artist/writer. Born and raised in Mexico City, he came to the United States in 1978. Since then he has been exploring cross-cultural issues with the use of performance, multilingual poetry, journalism, video, radio and installation art. He is a contributing editor to *High Performance Magazine* and *The Drama Review.* A collection of his writings, *Warrior for Gringostroika,* was recently published by Greywolf Press. *Borderless Radio,* an anthology of his audio work on CD was released in 1994 by Word of Mouth (Toronto, Canada).

Elena Poniatowska is the author of *Massacre in Mexico* (University of Missouri Press, 1991), an accounting of the student uprising of 1968 in Mexico, among many other books. She lives in Mexico City and writes articles for various publications, including *La Jornada.*

Yolanda Castro is an adviser to the Regional Union of Craftswomen of Chiapas in San Cristóbal, Chiapas.

SAIIC (South and Meso American Indian Information Center) is an organization which promotes peace and social justice for Indian peoples (see listing in Organizations).

Neyra P. Alvarado Solís was born in Michoacan and graduated from the National School of Anthropology and History, specializing in Ethnology. Her studies of the traditional medicinal practices of the Mixe Indians of Oaxaca was included in the prize-winning documentary, "Heal Me With Your Power." Her documentary "Asking for Life" is a study of orality and ritual of the Mexicanero Indians of Durango. She is the co-author of two books published by the National Indigenous Institute and the National Institute of Anthropology and History.

Vivian Newdick works with CONPAZ (Co-ordination of Non-governmental Organizations of Chiapas for Peace) , a recently formed coalition of women's, campesino, public health, religious, human rights, and development organizations in Chiapas. She lives in San Cristóbal, Chiapas.

Leonard Peltier is a Lakota Sioux who was active in the American Indian Movement in the 1970s. He is now imprisoned for life, falsely accused of shooting two FBI agents on the Pine Ridge Reservation in 1975. There is a branch of the Leonard Peltier Defense Committee, which coordinates action for his release, in most major cities.

Ward Churchill, an enrolled member of the United Keetoowah Band of Cherokees, is an Associate Professor of American Indian Studies and Communications at the University of Colorado, Boulder, where he serves as Associate Director of the Center for the Study of Ethnicity and Race in America. Since 1983, he has served on the Governing Council of the American Indian Movement of Colorado. Among his dozen books are: *Marxism and Native Americans* (1983), *Fantasies of the Master Race* (1992), and *Struggle for the Land* (1993).

Peter Rosset is Executive Director of the Institute for Food and Development Policy — Food First, based in Oakland, California. He is a leading specialist in Latin American rural development issues and is the author of *Nicaragua: Unfinished Revolution* (Grove Press, 1986) and *The Greening of the Revolution: Cuba's Experiment with Organic Agriculture* (Ocean Press, 1994). He also served as Executive Director of the Stanford University Regional Center in Chiapas, Mexico.

Iain A. Boal is a social historian of science and technics. He teaches at Stanford University, and is a co-editor of *Resisting the Virtual Life: The Culture and Politics of Information* (City Lights Books, 1995).

Noam Chomsky is a professor of Modern Languages and Linguistics at MIT. He is a leading spokesperson for the American Left, and the author of many books of analysis of United States foreign policy, most recently, *World Orders, Old and New* (Columbia University Press, 1994).

Jack D. Forbes is a professor and chair of Native American Studies at University of California, Davis. He is an internationally recognized scholar, poet, fiction writer, and community worker. Forbes, of Powhatan, Lenápe-Delaware, and other Native and European ancestry, is a co-founder of D-Q University and was one of the pioneers in the movement for Native American Studies as a discipline. His recent publications include: *Only Approved Indians, Africans and Native Americans,* and *Columbus and Other Cannibals.*

M. A. Jaimes Guerrero is an enrolled Juaneño/Yaqui, and has been a member of the Indigenous Women's Network, Colorado AIM, and the American Indian Anti-Defamation Council. She served as a delegate for the International Indian Treaty Council to the UN Working Group on Indigenous Populations. She is a professor in the Department of Justice Studies at Arizona State University. She has published numerous articles and essays on Native rights issues and is the editor of *The State of Native America: Genocide Colonization and Resistance* (South End Press), and the author of *Academic Apartheid in America* (Common Courage Press).

Juan Bañuelos was born in Tuxtla Gutierrez, Chiapas in 1932, the grandson of General Felix J. Bañuelos, who rode with Pancho Villa in the Mexican Revolution and was later governor of Zacatecas. In 1960, his first book, *Puertas al mundo,* was published in a collection of five poets, *La Espiga Amotinada.* He received the National Prize for Poetry, Certamen de Aguascalientes, in 1968. His work has been translated into many languages, and he is a contributor to national and international literary magazines and journals.

Eraclio Zepeda, poet and storyteller, was born in Chiapas in 1937. He has published five books of poetry, collected in the volume *Relación de travesía.* His books of stories include: *Benzulul, Asalto nocturno* and *Andando el tiempo.* He has received the National Short Story Prize, the Villarrutia Prize and the Chiapas Prize for Literature. He is currently the director of Radio UNAM. From January — August, 1994 he was a member of the Special Autonomous Commission for Peace in Chiapas, which facilitated peace negotiations between the Mexican government and the Zapatista Army. He is a member of the National Mediation Commission, continuing the work toward a negotiated settlement with the EZLN.

Leslie Marmon Silko is an acclaimed poet, novelist, and essayist. She was raised at Laguna Pueblo, and now lives in Tucson, Arizona. Among her many books are: *Almanac of the Dead (*Viking Penguin, 1992*), Ceremony (*Viking Penguin, 1986*),* and *Sacred Water (*Flood Plain Press, 1993).

Alberto Blanco is an internationally renowned poet, musician, translator, and art critic from Mexico City. His most recent books include *Los astros al otro lado del río,* a collection of translations of

North American poetry, and a collection of his own poems, *Cuenta de los guías*. He teaches in El Paso, Texas.

Antonio García de León is the author of many books and articles about anthropology, linguistics, history, and economics in Mexico. His work on Chiapas, including *Los elementos del tzotzil colonial y moderno, Ejército de ciegos: testimonios de la guerra chiapaneca entre carrancistas y rebeldes*, and his two-volume history *Resistencia y utopia*, is an authoritative source of information on the culture and history of the region. He is a member of the National Institute of Anthropology and History, and a coordinating member of the National Democratic Convention, a political organization of activists and intellectuals that was formed as a result of the conflict in Chiapas.

Ronnie Burk is a poet and collagist, born April Fools Day, 1955 in south Texas to a working class Anglo-Mexicano family. A recent contributor to *Caliban, City Lights Review, Cover (NY), Exquisite Corpse* and *Verbal Abuse*, his caustic obituary of Richard Nixon was included in a special issue of the *Radical History Review* (Nov., 1994).

Mongo Sánchez Lira and Rogelio Villarreal are the editors of *Pusmoderna*, a Mexico City magazine of alternative culture. They are also contributors to various reviews and magazines, including *La Jornada Semanal*.

Jack Hirschman is a poet and translator. His most recent publications include: *The Xibalba Arcane* (Azul Editions, 1994), a long poem of contemporary street life in the U.S., perceived within a Mayan context; and *The Sea on Its Side* (Post-Apollo Press, 1994), translations of the poetry of Ambar Past, a native of San Cristóbal de las Casas.

Elva Macías is a poet from Tuxtla Gutierrez, Chiapas. She is a fellow of the Centro Mexicano de Escritores [Mexican Center for Writers] and has published many books of poetry. Her most recent book, *Ciudad contra el cielo,*won the 1994 Carlos Pellicer Prize for Poetry. In 1993, she was awarded the Chiapas Prize for Literature. Her work appears in anthologies in Mexico and the United States.

Ignacio Nuñez Pliego is a free-lance journalist and photographer. He has contributed to various Mexican periodicals, including *Reforma, Proceso*, and *La Jornada*.

Lorenzo Armendariz is a prize-winning photographer whose work has been exhibited throughout Mexico and abroad, and published in numerous magazines in Mexico. Originally from Tamaulipas, he has worked for over 10 years with indigenous groups on the border and in the Los Altos region of Chiapas. His photographic archive in the National Indigenous Institute consists of over 35,000 images of approximately 30 indigenous groups of Mexico. He is a member of the Mexican Council of Photography.

David Maung is a photographer from Oakland, California, whose work documents social movements, political events, and the changing economic and cultural landscape in Mexico.

For more information, or to become actively involved, the following is a partial list of organizations:

Global Exchange
2017 Mission Street, Suite 303
San Francisco, CA 94110
phone: (415) 255-7296/(800) 497-1994

Global Exchange is an organization dedicated to grassroots development and international cooperation, founded in 1988. They have recently formed the U.S. – Mexico Partnership for Development, an alliance with several non-governmental organizations in Chiapas, working toward peaceful solutions to the conflict and to alleviate the poverty of the region. This includes support for repatriation for people displaced by the conflict, an organic gardening project, medicines and volunteer health professionals, seed money for expansion of women's craft cooperatives, and help for an indigenous radio station. In addition, Global Exchange sponsors a series of educational travel seminars from the U.S. to Chiapas and other impoverished regions, and speaking tours of Mexican development experts and activists to the United States. The organization regularly produces informational materials, recently, the *Chiapas Reader* and *Mexico Elections Reader*.

South and Meso American Indian Information Center
P.O. Box 28703
Oakland, CA 94604
phone: (510) 834-4263
fax: (510) 834-4264
email: igc.saiic

The South and Meso American Indian Rights Center (SAIIC) promotes peace and social justice for Indian people by providing information to people in the U.S. and the international community about the struggles of South and Meso American Indian people for self-determination, human rights, and protection of the environment. SAIIC also assists people in South and Meso America to gain access to international resources. *Abya Yala News*, SAIIC's quarterly newsletter, is available with an annual membership, and is also sold in bookstores.

Inter-Hemispheric Education Resource Center
Box 4506
Albuquerque, NM 87196
phone: (505) 842-8288
fax: (505) 246-1601

Since 1979, the Resource Center has produced books, policy reports, audiovisuals, and other educational materials about United States foreign relations with Mexico, Central America, and the Caribbean, as well as sponsoring popular education projects. They are a leading source of information for activists, organizers, legislators, and people interested in a more just U.S. policy abroad. The U.S. – Mexico Series is a collection of four books that examine the evolving relationship between our two countries, and its fundamental issues and problems. The *Resource Center Bulletin* is available by subscription, as is the quarterly newsletter, *Borderlines*.

Institute for Food and Development Policy/Food First
398 60th Street
Oakland, CA 94618
phone: (510) 654-4400
fax: (510) 654-4551

Food First is a nonprofit research and education-for-action center that investigates the root causes of hunger in a world of plenty. Founded in 1975, the Institute publishes books and bulletins that survey social conditions and development problems through a "food window." They also publish a series of Action Alerts, Development Reports, and Policy Briefs that provide the media, policy-makers, and the public with information and analysis on contemporary issues, most recently, *Land, Liberty and Food in Chiapas*, by Roger Burbach & Peter Rosset.

Equipo Pueblo
Apartado Postal 27-467
06760 Mexico, D.F.
phone: 011-525-539-0015
fax: 011-525-627-7453
email: pueblo@planeta.igc.apc.org

Equipo Pueblo is a Mexican non-governmental organization founded in 1977 as a popular education team. It works closely with popular movements and citizen coalitions in the promotion of democracy, the defense of human rights and the advancement of economic justice. Their bimonthly newsletter, *La otra cara de México/The Other Side of Mexico* is available by subscription.

Open Magazine Pamphlet Series
PO Box 2726
Westfield, NJ 07091-2726
phone: (908) 789-9608
fax: (908) 654-3829
email: opengrss@maestro.com

Open Magazine publishes a series of dissident essays, by and for activists, historians and scholars. *NAFTA, GATT, and the World Trade Organization*, by Kristin Dawkins & Jeremy Brecher; and *The Zapatistas, Starting from Chiapas*, by Marc Cooper, are recommended titles. For a free list of available titles, contact the publishers. The pamphlets are also sold in bookstores.

Love and Rage
PO Box 853
New York, NY 10009
phone: (718) 834-9077
email: lnr@blythe.org

Love and Rage is an anarchist newspaper which has covered the Zapatista uprising from the beginning. It is available by subscription or in local bookstores. They also publish *Amor y Rabia* in Mexico City.

Akwesasne Notes
P.O. Box 196
Rooseveltown, NY 13683-0196

Published for over twenty-five years, Akwesasne Notes is an international news voice for the Mohawk people and other Native people in North America. Written, produced and distributed from the Mohawk Nation Community of Akwesasne, the "Notes" dedicates each issue to stories such as Indian Treaty Rights, cultural activities, political actions and environmental issues. Published bimonthly and available in bookstores.

Suggestions for Further Reading:

Voice of Fire, Ben Clarke & Clifton Ross, eds., New Earth
   Publications, 1994.
   A selection of Zapatista communiqués and interviews.

Zapatistas! Documents of the New Mexican Revolution, Autonomedia
   Press, 1994.
   A complete collection of the Zapatista declarations, commu-
   niqués, and letters from December 31, 1993 — June 12, 1994.

Basta! Land and the Zapatista Rebellion in Chiapas, by George Collier,
   Food First Books, 1994.
   Outlines the local, national and international forces that created
   the situation in Chiapas. Thoroughly documented, comprehensive background to the revolution, with many individual
   accounts of struggle.

Rebellion from the Roots; Indian Uprising in Chiapas, by John Ross,
   Common Courage Press, 1995.
   Chronicles the Zapatista revolution, through the elections, and
   covers the history of indigenous and agrarian popular movements in Mexico.

Zapata's Revenge, by Tom Barry with Harry Browne, South End Press,
   1994.
   Presents a broad overview of land, hunger, agricultural production, and rural development issues in Mexico.

Mexican Lives, by Judith Adler Hellman, The New Press, 1994.
   A collection of profiles of fifteen Mexicans with a concise pre-
   sentation of recent Mexican economic and political history.
   Explores the effects of economic and political change in Mexico,
   including NAFTA, providing a context for the rebellion in
   Chiapas.

CITY LIGHTS PUBLICATIONS

Eidus, Janice. VITO LOVES GERALDINE
Fenollosa, Ernest. CHINESE WRITTEN CHARACTER AS A MEDIUM
    FOR POETRY
Ferlinghetti, Lawrence. PICTURES OF THE GONE WORLD
Ferlinghetti, L., ed. ENDS & BEGINNINGS (City Lights Review #6)
Finley, Karen. SHOCK TREATMENT
Ford, Charles Henri. OUT OF THE LABYRINTH: Selected Poems
Franzen, Cola, transl. POEMS OF ARAB ANDALUSIA
García Lorca, Federico. BARBAROUS NIGHTS: Legends & Plays
García Lorca, Federico. ODE TO WALT WHITMAN &
    OTHER POEMS
García Lorca, Federico. POEM OF THE DEEP SONG
Gil de Biedma, Jaime. LONGING: SELECTED POEMS
Ginsberg, Allen. THE FALL OF AMERICA
Ginsberg, Allen. HOWL & OTHER POEMS
Ginsberg, Allen. KADDISH & OTHER POEMS
Ginsberg, Allen. MIND BREATHS
Ginsberg, Allen. PLANET NEWS
Ginsberg, Allen. PLUTONIAN ODE
Ginsberg, Allen. REALITY SANDWICHES
Goethe, J. W. von. TALES FOR TRANSFORMATION
Hayton-Keeva, Sally, ed. VALIANT WOMEN IN WAR AND EXILE
Heider, Ulrike. ANARCHISM: Left Right & Green
Herron, Don. THE DASHIELL HAMMETT TOUR: A Guidebook
Herron, Don. THE LITERARY WORLD OF SAN FRANCISCO
Higman, Perry, tr. LOVE POEMS FROM SPAIN AND
    SPANISH AMERICA
Jaffe, Harold. EROS: ANTI-EROS
Jenkins, Edith. AGAINST A FIELD SINISTER
Katzenberger, Elaine, ed. FIRST WORLD, HA HA HA!
Kerouac, Jack. BOOK OF DREAMS
Kerouac, Jack. POMES ALL SIZES
Kerouac, Jack. SCATTERED POEMS
Kerouac, Jack. SCRIPTURE OF THE GOLDEN ETERNITY
Lacarrière, Jacques. THE GNOSTICS
La Duke, Betty. COMPAÑERAS
La Loca. ADVENTURES ON THE ISLE OF ADOLESCENCE
Lamantia, Philip. MEADOWLARK WEST
Laughlin, James. SELECTED POEMS: 1935–1985
Le Brun, Annie. SADE: On the Brink of the Abyss
Lowry, Malcolm. SELECTED POEMS
Mackey, Nathaniel. SCHOOL OF UDHRA
Marcelin, Philippe-Thoby. THE BEAST OF THE HAITIAN HILLS
Masereel, Frans. PASSIONATE JOURNEY
Mayakovsky, Vladimir. LISTEN! EARLY POEMS
Mrabet, Mohammed. THE BOY WHO SET THE FIRE
Mrabet, Mohammed. THE LEMON
Mrabet, Mohammed. LOVE WITH A FEW HAIRS

N

W CITY LIGHTS PUBLISHERS AND BOOKSELLERS E

S

CITY LIGHTS MAIL ORDER
Order books from our free catalog:

all books from
CITY LIGHTS PUBLISHERS
and more

write to:
CITY LIGHTS MAIL ORDER
261 COLUMBUS AVENUE
SAN FRANCISCO, CA 94133
or fax your request to
[415] 362-4921